JOHN F. KENNEDY

MAKERS OF AMERICA

JOHN F. KENNEDY:
PORTRAIT OF A PRESIDENT

MARTIN S. GOLDMAN

Facts On File®

AN INFOBASE HOLDINGS COMPANY

John F. Kennedy: Portrait of a President

Facts On File, Inc.
460 Park Avenue South
New York NY 10016

Library of Congress Cataloging-in-Publication Data
Goldman, Martin S.
    John F. Kennedy, portrait of a president / by Martin S. Goldman.
      p. cm. — (Makers of America)
    Includes bibliographical references and index.
    ISBN 0-8160-3243-2
    1. Kennedy, John F. (John Fitzgerald), 1917–1963. 2. Presidents—
United States—Biography. I. Title. II. Series: Makers of
America (Facts On File, Inc.)
E842.G55 1995
973.922'092—dc20
[B]   94-36494

Text design by Debbie Glasserman
Jacket design by Duane Stapp

Printed in the United States of America

RRD FOF 10 9 8 7 6 5 4 3 2 1

This book is printed on acid-free paper.

*To Ann: for lots of bagels, coffee
and much love*

CONTENTS

ACKNOWLEDGMENTS

M y historical relationship with John F. Kennedy goes way back to that tragic weekend in November 1963 when, as a grief-stricken young history teacher, I first put some thoughts onto paper. JFK was my first real president. I turned 21 on election day in 1960 and proudly cast my first vote for JFK. He became the keystone of my entire generation, and his untimely death changed many of our lives and too much of American history. Yet, despite all that has been written and said about him, we still don't really know him. The JFK legend and myth, fostered by his late widow and his many friends, far exceeds any current reality—especially among Democrats around election time.

At any rate, in 1963 I screwed up my courage and shared my thoughts with my friend Alvin's mother. The late Annie Kolchins was not, as I recall, a woman who ever minced words. "Marty Goldman," she said, "you should be a writer." And mostly, among other things in this life, that is what I am. So, my first debt for this book is to Annie Kolchins, the first person to read anything I wrote and the first person to offer me the vital encouragement that every writer needs. Thanks, Annie!

There are, of course, many others. At Boston University, Michael Kort, who teaches history, is one of my most cherished friends, allies and critics. Mike (and his wife Carol) have always been there for me over the years. Professor Joseph Boskin gave me the opportunity to teach "The Kennedy Presidency" at Boston University's Metropolitan College and to work out some of my views in a classroom setting. My students at Boston University, on campus and at MCI–Norfolk and Bay State (the state prisons), constantly challenged me to build on lectures and classroom discussion. This book is the result. The unwavering friendship of Larry Lowenthal in Boston and Larry Laster in Philadelphia has been an important part of my life. At the John F. Kennedy Library, Sheldon Stern has always been helpful and wise.

At Facts On File I am indebted to James Warren and to my most able and helpful editor, John Anthony Scott. My parents, Louis and Ruth Goldman, my Aunt Nan Praisman and my brother, Ken Goldman, a dedicated teacher and a very creative writer in his own right, have always been wonderfully supportive.

Finally, there should always be a dog. Wookie has been my constant and faithful companion, patiently snoozing by my computer in my study in peaceful Sudbury. His like shall never pass this way again.

INTRODUCTION
Inauguration Day, January 20, 1961

> "Ask not what your country can do for you . . ."

The day of January 20, 1961 was so bitter cold in Washington, D.C. that people on the streets could see their breath in great puffs of white every time they spoke. The temperature was barely 22 icy degrees above zero.

Many who stood in the large crowds that lined Pennsylvania Avenue all the way to Capitol Hill stamped their feet to keep them from freezing as they lingered in the eager anticipation that they soon might catch a glance of the man they had been waiting to see for hours. It had snowed very hard the night before, but the government workmen had labored all through the cold night to clear Pennsylvania Avenue for the inaugural parade—a parade that was held only once every four years, after the fall presidential election.

When the snow stopped shortly before dawn, Washington, D.C. had turned into a city of bright and glittering white. It was almost as if the city had cleaned itself up to put the tired and stodgy decade of the 1950s into the past once and for all. It seemed as though the city and the people understood that the country was standing on the threshold of a promising new era that was about to begin with a youthful presidential air of hope and vigor.

Shortly before noon the president-elect, who hadn't slept much the night before, and his attractive young wife met with the outgoing president of the United States, Dwight David Eisenhower, and his vice president, Richard M. Nixon, who had been defeated in the fierce contest for the presidency the previous November, and their wives. They gathered in the Red Room of the White House for coffee and small talk before leaving for the Capitol, where the new president would be sworn in by the chief justice of the United States Supreme Court.

Soon the presidential party put on their top hats and formal waistcoats and entered the long, sleek black limousines for the short drive along Pennsylvania Avenue to the Capitol.

Under a blue and cloudless sky, the crowds of eager Americans in their heavy winter clothes watched, waited and shivered. The cold was relentless but the anticipation was warming.

One by one the political dignitaries arrived at the large platform in front of the Capitol building. They got out of their limos and nervously acknowledged the throngs of people as they took their seats on the platform.

At 20 minutes past noon the president-elect, now hatless, appeared and was greeted with warming applause from the crowds. They listened quietly as His Eminence, Richard Cardinal Cushing, the president-elect's old family friend who had once been a parish priest in Boston, gave a long invocation in his familiar raspy voice.

The famous poet Robert Frost, somewhat blinded by the intense glare of the sun over the newly fallen snow, recited his poem "The Gift Outright" from memory in a halting voice as the vice president-elect held out his hat to shield the white-haired old man from the bright sun. Frost had originally begun to read another poem. But after reading three lines from his manuscript, he still could not see, and thus he switched to a poem that he knew by heart and therefore did not have to read.

Shortly before one o'clock, Chief Justice Earl Warren stepped forward to administer the oath of office. The president-elect put his hand on an old Bible that had been handed down in the Fitzgerald family and responded to the chief justice in a firm voice. Then he began his inaugural address, electrifying the crowd and the nation with those unforgettable words in the frosty early afternoon air.[1]

> Let the word go forth from this time and place, to friend and foe alike, that the torch has been passed to a new generation of Americans—born in this century, tempered by war, disciplined by a hard and bitter peace, proud of our ancient heritage—and unwilling to witness or permit the

slow undoing of those human rights to which this nation has always been committed, and to which we are committed today at home and around the world.

Let every nation know, whether it wishes us well or ill, that we shall pay any price, bear any burden, meet any hardship, support any friend, oppose any foe to assure the survival and the success of liberty.

This much we pledge and more.[2]

The new president, however, didn't want to frighten the foreign leaders he knew would be listening carefully to his words. So he took the opportunity to add words to his address that would make it unmistakably clear that the United States of America sought peace even though the nation would remain militarily strong. He said,

So let us begin anew—remembering on both sides that civility is not a sign of weakness, and sincerity is always subject to proof. Let us never negotiate out of fear. But let us never fear to negotiate.[3]

He warned his fellow citizens that the road ahead would not be smooth. And he wanted them to know that the burden would not be only his. Once again in this most dangerous century in world history, Americans were being called upon to carry the weight of a precarious world. Noting that the tasks of world leadership would take time to accomplish, the new president said,

All this will not be finished in the first 100 days. Nor will it be finished in the first 1,000, nor in the life of this Administration, nor even perhaps in our lifetime on this planet. But let us begin.

. . . And so, my fellow Americans, ask not what your country can do for you—ask what you can do for your country.

My fellow citizens of the world: ask not what America will do for you, but what together we can do for the freedom of man.[4]

The crowds cheered as he left the platform, and his wife touched his face tenderly as the inaugural parade slowly made its way back up Pennsylvania Avenue to the White House in the freezing cold of the waning afternoon.

At 42 he was the youngest man ever elected to the presidency of the United States or even nominated by the Democratic Party. He was a Roman Catholic, and no member of that faith had ever even been considered for the presidency since Governor Al Smith of New York had been defeated in 1928. It was thought that no Catholic could ever be elected president of the United States. But he had proved that notion to be wrong.

He had been a United States senator from Massachusetts, and in the country's history only one senator—a Republican— had ever been elected president. The Democrats in the House had favored Senator Stuart Symington of Missouri. Senate Democrats had backed Senator Lyndon Baines Johnson of Texas, the Senate majority leader—as had the party leadership. Former candidate Adlai Stevenson, who had once been governor of Illinois and had twice run unsuccessfully against Eisenhower, in 1952 and 1956, had favored himself. Newspaper editors and college professors, America's intellectual elite, had backed Stevenson, with a few exceptions among those who had known Kennedy when he was a student at Harvard.

Many of his critics believed that Kennedy was too young, and too inexperienced, and that his lackluster record in Congress did not entitle him to lead the nation in such troubled times. It was the height of the ongoing struggle between Russia and the United States that was known as the cold war. Indeed, it was a dangerous time.

Yet he had won the nomination of his party, and had beaten a sitting vice president, and he became the first president of the United States who was born in the 20th century. If nothing else, his election marked the beginning of a new era of American history. It was to be a time of great optimism and hope. It was a time when it felt good to be an American.

He was energetic, vigorous and handsome. He had a smart, stylish and beautiful young wife and a large, closely knit family that he trusted implicitly.

He became the first politician in the country's history to effectively use television, which was just emerging from its own electronic infancy. And yet, when he was elected in November 1960, few Americans really knew John F. Kennedy.

Today many politicians celebrate his life and his presidency. He is almost always recalled by Democrats who want to remind voters that they will bring youth, creativity and vigor to the White House. Who will ever forget Senator Lloyd Bentsen blasting Senator Dan Quayle in the 1988 vice-presidential debate after Quayle made the mistake of comparing himself to John F. Kennedy? Senator Bentsen, bridling at the comparison, focused on the hapless Quayle, who looked like a frightened deer caught in the glare of an automobile's headlights. Fixing Quayle with an icy stare, Bentsen said, "Senator, I served with Jack Kennedy. Jack Kennedy was a friend of mine. Senator, you're no Jack Kennedy." [5]

Who was John Fitzgerald Kennedy? Where did he come from? What did his short presidency of a little more than a thousand days accomplish? And most important, stripping aside the rumors and the myths about his life and his death, what is his rightful place in the history of the United States?

Notes

1. Arthur M. Schlesinger, Jr., *A Thousand Days: John F. Kennedy in the White House* (Boston, 1965), pp. 1–4.
2. Davis Newton Lott, *The Presidents Speak: The Inaugural Addresses of the American Presidents from Washington to Nixon* (New York, 1969), p. 269.
3. Ibid., p. 270.
4. Ibid., p. 271.
5. Peter Goldman and Tom Mathews, *The Quest for the Presidency: The 1988 Campaign* (New York, 1989), p. 383.

1

BEGINNINGS—JFK'S EARLY LIFE

John Fitzgerald Kennedy was born on May 29, 1917, at home on Beals Street in Brookline, Massachusetts, an attractive streetcar suburb of Boston. The second son of Joseph P. Kennedy and Rose Fitzgerald Kennedy, young John F. Kennedy was born into a world of wealth and comfort that few of his fellow Irish Catholics enjoyed in and around the greater Boston area—an area that had been heavily settled by poor Irish immigrants since the middle of the 19th century.

The Kennedys and Fitzgeralds of Boston had deep roots in the political life of the old city. Rose Kennedy's father, John Francis Fitzgerald, known to all his political cronies as "Honey Fitz," had been elected to Congress for three terms between 1894 and 1900. He was thwarted for a fourth term by an old political enemy, Patrick J. Kennedy, John F. Kennedy's paternal grandfather, who had made a comfortable living as a saloonkeeper in East Boston.

Life had never been easy for the Boston Irish. They had suffered from a degree of prejudice and discrimination that some have compared to the bigotry experienced by black Americans. A quick glance at the employment advertisements in almost any Boston newspaper after the Civil War will show one job listing after another that included the line, "No Irish Need Apply." Thus, many Irish-Americans saw politics as one of the few avenues for the much-despised and discriminated-against Irish immigrants and their children to rise to wealth and power in American society during this period—a time in American history often called "the Gilded Age." As former Speaker of the House Thomas P. "Tip" O'Neill recalled, "I knew I was Irish even before I knew I was American." It was Speaker

O'Neill, a veteran Boston politician, who coined the phrase "All politics is local."[1]

And it was in the "local" politics of Irish Boston that the Kennedy and Fitzgerald families often clashed. The intense competition for political power between the Kennedys and the Fitzgeralds came to a head in the tough mayoral contest of 1905, when Honey Fitz outwitted Patrick J. Kennedy's candidate. Honey Fitz was elected mayor of Boston by almost 4,000 votes.[2]

Romance, however, intervened. When Patrick J. Kennedy's son, young Joseph P. Kennedy, who had been born in 1888, met Rose Fitzgerald, the beautiful daughter of the mayor, in the summer of 1906 during a family vacation in Old Orchard Beach, Maine, the political rivalry of the two families was finally put to rest. At first, Mayor Fitzgerald tried to discourage his pretty daughter from any involvement at all with the brash young Joe Kennedy. The mayor of Boston had no desire to see his precious Rose, whose life he had tightly controlled even to the point of preventing her from attending a secular school like Wellesley College, marry into the hated Kennedy family. Rose Fitzgerald Kennedy remembered, "I suppose no father thinks any man is good enough for his daughter. My father had extravagant notions of my beauty, grace, wit, and charm. As I entered young womanhood these delusions deepened."[3]

For young Joe Kennedy, money had never been a major problem. His family had become affluent enough to send him to the intensely competitive Protestant world of Harvard University, where he had graduated in 1912.

But the long political rivalry between the Fitzgeralds and the Kennedys slowly melted away in the face of romance and courtship. It ultimately disappeared altogether when the two families were finally united with the marriage of Joseph P. Kennedy to Rose Elizabeth Fitzgerald on October 7, 1914. The couple were married in a traditional Catholic ritual, but certainly not by a traditional parish priest. The ceremony was performed by William Cardinal O'Connell in his exclusive private chapel, with only the immediate members of the two politically powerful Boston Irish families in attendance.[4]

After his marriage, young Joseph Kennedy concentrated his energies on making as much money as he could as quickly as possible. By the time Joseph P. Kennedy was 25 he had become the youngest bank president in the nation. "I want to be a millionaire by the age of thirty-five," he told his friends.[5] He clearly understood that great wealth could be a useful tool to lift himself and his family to a prominent position in the heady social and political whirl of Boston and, later, in the political life of the entire nation.

From local banking, after World War I, Joe Kennedy diversified his business interests, turning westward to the allure of big money and pretty women in the new motion picture industry that was rapidly developing in Hollywood, California. Meanwhile, his family was also developing.

After the birth of Joe Jr. in 1915 and John in 1917, other children followed in rapid succession. In September 1918, Rosemary was born; and in 1920 Kathleen arrived. The young Kennedy family was growing so quickly that the modest house at 83 Beals Street was no longer adequate. Shortly after Kathleen's birth the Kennedys moved into a larger house on the corner of Naples and Abbottsford Road, a few blocks away from Beals Street. There in 1921, another daughter, Eunice, was born. To help her cope with her growing family, Rose hired a nurse and a governess. John F. Kennedy was probably never a lonely child growing up in a home with so many children always around him. But the sporadic absence of both parents must have had some effect.[6] In 1919, trouble loomed for the young Kennedy family when the father took a seat in the Milk Street office of the stockbrokerage Hayden, Stone and Company in Boston. Now, Joe Kennedy was constantly either working or traveling on business. Rose Kennedy recalled, "He was under such pressure that, except for Sundays, he came home just long enough to sleep."[7]

One Kennedy relative, recalling the early years of the Kennedy marriage when John F. Kennedy was just a child, said, "Even in the early years of their marriage, Joe had a reputation for being a ladies man, and some of this gossip must have caught up with Rose."

Early in 1920, Rose, fed up with her husband's prolonged absences and cheating with other women, left her young children and returned to her parents' home in Dorchester for three weeks. Rose's father urged her to return to her family. "You've made your commitment, Rosie, and you must honor it now. What is past is past. The old days are gone. Your children need

Joseph and Rose Kennedy with their growing family. John F. Kennedy is at bottom left. (National Park Service)

you and your husband needs you. You can make things work out. . . . So go now, Rosie, go back where you belong," John F. Fitzgerald told his cherished daughter.[8]

Rose Kennedy, to her credit, went home to her three children and her husband. And she never again publicly complained about her lot in life. She busied herself with extensive traveling, with her church, and with the more formal duties of running a growing household that eventually included nine boisterous and competitive children.

Among the many affairs Joe Kennedy is said to have carried on with other women was a widely rumored romance with the famous silent screen star Gloria Swanson in the late 1920s—a romance that was considered very scandalous at the time because Swanson was also married. Kennedy denied the affair throughout his life. However, Swanson confirmed their extra-marital relationship in her autobiography, published shortly before she died in 1980.[9]

Young John F. Kennedy could hardly have escaped the serious emotional effects of the glaring dysfunction that existed within his large and growing family. His father was constantly away from home on business or chasing after women, and his mother was either pregnant or preoccupied with her own travels—her way of forgetting the problems she faced on the home front.

To add to his burdens, John F. Kennedy was often a sickly child. In February 1920, shortly after Rose Kennedy returned to her home and family, her second son, John, or "Jack" as he was called by everyone, fell deathly ill with scarlet fever.

Scarlet fever, a dangerous disease known to strike young children, is characterized by a sudden high fever, sometimes rising as high as 105 degrees in the initial hours, with accompanying problems of a sore throat, swollen tonsils, puffiness in the face, and a raging scarlet rash that spreads over the entire body. Normally, the fever subsides and the rash fades after four or five days. But in John F. Kennedy's case the illness was particularly intense, and after a week neither the rash nor the fever had diminished. The youngster was not even three years old.

This, the first of many illnesses to shadow John F. Kennedy's life, was clearly life-threatening, and for a time the Kennedys did not expect their son to live. A priest was called in to pray, and Joe Kennedy, convinced that his son was dying, offered to give half of his fortune to the church if somehow his son's life could be saved.

Jack's illness plunged the Kennedy household into what Rose later described as a state of "frantic terror." With Rose Kennedy recovering from the birth of her second daughter Kathleen, it was left to her husband to step into the crisis caused by young John's illness. Scarlet fever was highly contagious, and the Kennedys worried that Joe Jr. and Rosemary would catch it, and that even baby Kathleen, born on February 20, was susceptible. In those days Brookline Hospital refused to admit patients with contagious diseases, and the Kennedys were not technically eligible to use city hospital facilities in Boston. But technicalities rarely stopped the Kennedys of Massachusetts from getting whatever they wanted or needed.

Once again it was Honey Fitz, Rose's father, who came to the rescue. He prevailed upon Dr. Edwin Place to admit his sick grandson to Boston City Hospital. There, under the care of Dr. Place and a bevy of nurses who grew to love the child, John F. Kennedy survived his first encounter with near death.

For his part, Joe Kennedy was devastated. He had never faced the all-consuming finality of the possible death of one of his children. He had clearly feared that his son was going to die. As Joe Kennedy wrote to Dr. Place:

> I had never experienced any very serious sickness in my family previous to Jack's and I little realized what an effect such a happening could possibly have on me. During the darkest days I felt that nothing else mattered except his recovery.[10]

Every morning Joe Kennedy would go to church to pray for his son John. And every afternoon, surprising many who knew him, he put all his business interests aside to visit his boy in the hospital, where he undoubtedly brought John F. Kennedy the kind of love and attention the boy had not known in the first two years of his young life. Finally, in March, the little boy's fever broke. Gradually, under the care of a loving hospital staff that constantly reassured Joe Kennedy that his son was "a wonderful boy," Jack Kennedy grew stronger. It would, however, be another four weeks before he could leave the hospital, and there were two additional weeks of recuperation in Maine. It wasn't until May that John F. Kennedy was allowed to return to his family in Brookline.

Jack's illness had the positive effect of bringing his parents closer together. As Rose recalled, "After Jack's illness, Joe was determined to keep up with every little thing the children were doing. Every night we would spend hours together talking about the family and going over the children's activities. It made me feel that I had a partner in my enterprise."[11]

A partner in Rose Kennedy's "enterprise" is exactly what Joe Kennedy became—at least in the enterprise of producing children. By the time her last child, Edward Moore Kennedy, was born in 1932, the Kennedy family had grown to nine children.

Kennedy family life in their various homes—in Boston and later in Hyannis and Palm Beach, Florida, where the Kennedys spent their winter vacations in a rambling Spanish-style home by the sea—was a study in family competition. The children were extremely close—especially Bobby, Pat, Jean and little Edward (called "Teddy"), who formed "best-friend" relationships as youngsters. The Kennedy children were always being tested by their parents, whether on the playing field or at the family dinner table, where they were quizzed about current events. It was what one Kennedy friend described as "rough love."

By the time John F. Kennedy was a teenager, an uneasy hierarchy had been formed in his family, with his elder brother Joe Jr. (also called "Young Joe") at the top. Because their parents were absent so often—one friend estimated that in the six years after Joseph Kennedy had returned from Hollywood, Rose Kennedy took some 17 trips abroad—Joe Jr. often took on the role of a substitute parent. "You know," Joe Jr. once told a friend, "I'm the oldest of my family and I've got to be the example for a lot of brothers and sisters."[12]

In the autumn of 1931 John F. Kennedy followed his older brother Joe to the exclusive private school Choate. He had already had a taste of boarding school at the Catholic Canterbury School in New Milford, Connecticut. Young Jack Kennedy always seemed to acquire decent grades in school, although his spelling, throughout his life, was never very good. As he wrote to his mother, "I learnt to play baggammon to-day," and "I will be quite pius [sic] when I get home."

At Choate, where Joe Jr. had already established himself as a big man on campus—as an athlete and as the editor of the school paper—young Jack hardly stood out among his schoolmates. His health was a constant problem. Although he did not do very well in subjects like Latin, French, math and English, he seemed to have a keen appreciation of his favorite subject, history. He also did very well in physics. He graduated from Choate in the middle of his class—65th out of a class of 110.[13]

That September, instead of starting college, Jack accompanied his parents and six siblings on a trip to London, where his father was to begin a six-week tour of the gold bloc countries.

Joseph Kennedy Sr. had recently resigned as chairman of the Securities and Exchange Commission (SEC). He had become an informal adviser to President Franklin D. Roosevelt, who had been struggling to lift the nation out of the worst depression in American history. The elder Kennedy had been rewarded with the SEC job for his financial and political support of Roosevelt in the 1932 presidential campaign. President Roosevelt, did not fully trust the ambitious millionaire, however, although he needed Kennedy's good will, his money and his many connections.

When he finally rewarded Joe Kennedy with the SEC position as top watchdog of the nation's financial markets, the president is said to have remarked, "Set a thief to catch a thief."[14]

At any rate, Jack's stay in London was to be short-lived. Following his eldest brother Joe Jr. to the London School of Economics, young Jack lasted only a few weeks. Although later biographers claimed that JFK spent a year at the prestigious school, the truth is that within a month his poor health had forced him to return home. His mother claimed that he had gotten hepatitis or jaundice. But whatever the disease was that afflicted John F. Kennedy at the age of 18, once back in the United States he chose to take late entry at Princeton University to be with his old Choate pals, K. LeMoyne Billings—known as Lem, the son of a Pittsburgh physician—and Ralph "Rip" Horton.

Billings was to become a lifelong friend of Jack Kennedy. At Choate, with about a dozen other boys, the two had started "the Muckers Club." The Muckers had always been at odds with the Choate School administrators and were notorious all over the school for playing pranks and tricks on the other students, instructors and administrators. JFK recalled his brief Princeton stay:

> Princeton? I didn't do much at Princeton. No,
> I didn't read much. It was mostly physical. Then
> I had jaundice.

Because of his recurring illness, Kennedy soon found himself a year behind his chum Lem Billings. Rather than play catch-up, Jack gave in to his father's formidable influence, which finally opened the doors of the elder Kennedy's alma mater. In the fall of 1936 young John F. Kennedy entered Harvard University. His College Board and Scholastic Aptitude Tests had averaged only a rather dismal 69 points—a figure that would have kept most young men from less powerful and influential families out of the most elite schools.

As at Choate, illness had once again determined young John F. Kennedy's fate. Poor Jack had been plagued by so much bad health that his younger brother Bobby humorously wrote, "If a mosquito bit Jack, the mosquito would die."[15]

At Harvard Jack wanted more than anything to be compared favorably with his brother Joe. He ran unsuccessfully for class president and also made the freshman football team, playing end in three games. Weighing only 149 pounds, Jack Kennedy was hardly intimidating on the football field, and he finally dropped the sport in his sophomore year when his back started to give him serious problems. Kennedy remembered, "Freshman year was mostly sports, football and swimming." The key to Kennedy character-building at Harvard seemed to be football. Like their father before them, all four Kennedy brothers played football at Harvard.[16]

At Harvard University, JFK's closest friends were mostly other athletes like the patrician Torbert (Torby) Macdonald, who would eventually go on to Congress and become a lifelong Kennedy friend and political ally.

Chasing young women also became one of Jack Kennedy's preoccupations while at Harvard. In a letter to Lem Billings, Kennedy wrote, "I am now known as Play-boy." His professors, in the first few years, were hardly impressed with John F. Kennedy as a student. John Kenneth Galbraith, the famous Harvard professor of economics who later became President Kennedy's ambassador to India, knew both Kennedy brothers well. He recalled Joe Kennedy as "every faculty's favorite" and Jack as "gregarious, irreverent . . . far from diligent. One did not cultivate such students."[17]

But like many bright young men stimulated by first-rate teachers and thinkers, John F. Kennedy woke up to the value of education. In between his second and third year at Harvard, with the situation in Europe once again moving perilously toward worldwide conflict, John F. Kennedy came alive as a student and found that he was deeply interested in foreign affairs. Jack personally gave little credit to his professors at Havard. He recalled:

> I guess it was during my sophomore year that I really found myself. I don't know what to attribute it to. No, not to my professors. I guess I was just getting older. It was

during my junior year that I went to England for six months, which meant taking six courses as a senior and hard work. I had to work like hell.[18]

In the summer of 1937 Jack went to Europe with Lem Billings and traveled through France, Germany, Italy and England. There was, of course, swimming, hiking, dating exotic young women and some gambling. But there was also a serious side to this student tour of Europe. Billings and Kennedy attended public speeches by the Italian fascist dictator Benito Mussolini, met refugees who had fled the Spanish Civil War and spoke with knowledgeable people who understood both communism and fascism. For the first time, it seemed that Jack Kennedy had begun to grapple with great ideas. He wrote to his father, "Fascism is the thing for Germany and Italy, Communism for Russia and democracy for America and England."[19]

By the end of the year President Roosevelt had named Joseph Kennedy ambassador to England to pay him back for his endorsement in the presidential election of 1936. The elder Kennedy had written a book entitled *I'm for Roosevelt.*

Although Joseph Kennedy asked that his two eldest sons advise him in his new post on an unofficial basis, in later years Jack Kennedy did his best to convince people that his influence on his father during those years had been minimal. "Don't forget," Jack Kennedy later said, "I went to Spain, I went to England, I traveled all over Europe on my own. He wasn't with me."[20]

As the war clouds gathered over Europe with the rise of Adolf Hitler and the Nazis in Germany, Ambassador Kennedy seemed to be going off in a direction that was not in accord with the policies of President Roosevelt. Although a small group of isolationists, led by the hero of the first solo nonstop transatlantic flight, Colonel Charles A. Lindbergh, called for American neutrality in dealing with the growing Nazi menace in Europe, the Roosevelt administration was moving rapidly to fight off the enveloping tentacles of the Nazi octopus. Initially, Ambassador Kennedy sided with Lindbergh and the forces that sought to appease Hitler and the Nazis. He gave a major speech at the Trafalgar Day dinner defending the infamous Munich Agreement of 1938. England's prime minister, Neville Chamberlain, had signed this treaty, which gave the Sudetenland to Germany for what Chamberlain naively called "peace in our time." He thus paved the way for the Nazis to take over all of Czechoslovakia just a few months later without firing a shot.[21]

Joseph Kennedy seemed to be moving toward isolationism just as his president and his nation were moving toward a more meaningful role in world affairs for the United States. Some historians have attributed Ambassador Kennedy's flirtation with the Nazis and with the views of Charles A. Lindbergh to the fact that Joseph Kennedy was an anti-Semite.

The elder Kennedy had always been known to make disparaging remarks against Jews, and by most standards he would be classified as an anti-Semite. His influence on his eldest son, Joe Jr., could be detected in Joe's letters to his father, which seemed to applaud the latest Nazi outrages. Joe Kennedy, Jr. would write:

> Hitler came in. He saw the need for a common enemy, someone of whom to make the goat . . . it was too bad that it had to be done to the Jews. This dislike of the Jews, however, was well-founded.

Accepting the typical stereotypes, distortions and lies that exemplify anti-Semitic thought, Joe assured his father that the Jews of Germany controlled big business, law and other prominent German institutions. The brutality of the Nazis, he continued, was

> necessary . . . to secure the whole-hearted support of the people, which was necessary to put through this present program. . . . It was a horrible thing but in every revolution you have to expect some bloodshed. Hitler is building a spirit in his men that could be envied in any country.[22]

There is no record that Ambassador Kennedy ever corrected his son's admiration for Adolf Hitler or his anti-Semitic views. Like his eldest son, the ambassador chose to see the Nazi regime's violent hatred of Jews as a method to encourage German economic growth and business expansion. As the German government prepared for all-out war against Great Britain, Ambassador Kennedy would say,

> The Germans probably feel that they have to preserve
> some apparently bitter external enemies in order to whip
> up their own people to the necessary sacrifices, and En-
> gland is cast in this role just now.[23]

Joseph Kennedy's flirtation with the Nazis, his stong belief
that they would win any European war, and his role in the
process of appeasement would ultimately ruin his career in
American politics. However, his casual anti-Semitism did not
make him into a Nazi. Ambassador Kennedy took little pleasure in the tragedy that was befalling the Jews of Germany
under Hitler and the Nazis. In the aftermath of the infamous
Kristallnacht (Night of Broken Glass) in November 1938 when
hundreds of Jews were murdered and thousands of Jewish
shops, businesses and synagogues were trashed, Ambassador
Kennedy tried to help German Jews escape from the impending
Holocaust that befell European Jewry.[24]

For his part, young John F. Kennedy did his best to distance
himself somewhat from the views of his brother and his famous
father. His father's anti-Semitism apparently had little impact
on him. He returned to Harvard in the fall of 1939 and made
B's in all his government and economics courses. To graduate
with an honors degree in political science, Jack Kennedy decided to write an undergraduate thesis on how the British had
appeased the Germans at Munich (the topic had been suggested, interestingly enough, by his father).

With the aid of a personal secretary and at least five stenog-
raphers, John F. Kennedy prepared the 150-page paper. The
thesis was very sympathetic to Prime Minister Chamberlain
and argued that there were complex reasons for England
caving in to the Nazis. His two faculty readers did not think
much of the analysis, or of the writing. The files at Harvard on
the Kennedy thesis note: "Badly written" and "Fundamental
premise never analyzed. . . . Many typographical errors." Curiously, it was accepted for *magna cum laude* and *cum laude
plus*. His brother Joe Jr. read it and did not think it was very
good. In a letter to his father, the eldest Kennedy brother wrote,
"It seemed to represent a lot of work but did not prove anything." [25]

Nevertheless, the ambassador urged Jack to send the thesis
to his good friend Arthur Krock of the *New York Times*. The

John F. Kennedy with his brothers Teddy on shoulders and Bobby (John F. Kennedy Library)

ambassador had been friends with Krock since 1932 and had often provided inside political information in return for favorable press coverage when Krock was Washington bureau chief. Joe Kennedy had even once tried to bribe Krock with the gift of an automobile—a gift the newspaperman wisely rejected. Krock helped with the editing and polishing of the Kennedy thesis and gave it a new title, "Why England Slept." Krock recalled,

> It was remarkable, not so much for the freshness and precision of the supporting data (since the facilities for this were readily available in the elder Kennedy's files) as for the fine perception of the fundamental problems of a peace-loving democracy threatened with dictatorial regimes bent on subversive annexation or war.[26]

With the help of Krock and of his father's personal speechwriter, the thesis was finally published as a book in late July of 1940 under the title *Why England Slept.* Ambassador Kennedy's close friend Henry Luce, the publisher of *Time* and *Life* magazines, wrote the introduction and saw to it that the book received a great deal of attention and publicity. Luce wrote, "I cannot recall a single man of my college generation who could have written such an adult book on such a vitally important subject during his senior year at college." Kennedy's father saw more important reasons for the publication of an important book. He wrote his son, "You would be surprised how a book that really makes the grade with high-class people stands you in good stead for years to come." With his picture next to a positive review in *Time,* and a main selection by the Book-of-the-Month Club, the book soon became a national best-seller. Of course, it did not hurt that his father had quietly purchased between 30,000 and 40,000 copies for discreet storage in the attic and basement at the Kennedy family home in Hyannis Port in Massachusetts.[27]

This book was only the first in a long line of books designed at critical junctures over the years to promote the name and political career of John F. Kennedy.

Timing was also an important factor in the book's success. It came out just as the German blitz of England—the air war the Germans had launched to crush the spirit of the British—had begun. By the spring of 1941, 80,000 copies of the Kennedy book had been sold, half of them being distributed in England. At only 23 years of age, John F. Kennedy was a published and respected author. In a nation rapidly becoming obsessed with the notion of celebrity and one where the media was beginning to wield power and influence unknown in a less technologically oriented age, John F. Kennedy stepped onto the national political stage just as he graduated from college.[28]

His father's many friends and influential contacts had helped to get his book published and widely publicized. At an age when most young men and women are just starting that great struggle with the awesome responsibilities of life and a career, John F. Kennedy had already become an acknowledged public figure. He had become something of a young superstar in the competitive world of letters without much effort, and with the help of the kind of Gatsby-like connections, entree and support few young Americans could ever even imagine or know.

As World War II closed in on an increasingly troubled, complex and dangerous world, it seemed that young John F. Kennedy was on his way. His rather simplistic views of recent current events that had led up to the war clouds that now thundered over Europe had thrust young Jack Kennedy into the public eye and into the arena of world affairs. Not a single political analyst, book reviewer or critic, however, ever stopped to ask the all-important question or even to wonder: on his way to what?

Notes

1. Thomas P. O'Neill with William Novak, *Man of the House* (New York, 1987), p. 7 and p. 26. See also Nigel Hamilton, *J.F.K.: Restless Youth* (New York, 1992), pp. 7–9; Thomas C. Reeves, *A Question of Character: A Life of John F. Kennedy* (New York, 1991), p. 19; Richard J. Whalen, *The Founding Father: The Story of Joseph P. Kennedy* (New York, 1964), p. 24.

2. Hamilton, *J.F.K.*, p. 15.

3. Ibid.; and quoted in Rose Fitzgerald Kennedy, *Times to Remember* (New York, 1974), p. 62.
4. Doris Kearns Goodwin, *The Fitzgeralds and the Kennedys: An American Saga* (New York, 1987), p. 259.
5. Reeves, *A Question of Character,* p. 22. See also Peter Collier and David Horowitz, *The Kennedys: An American Drama* (New York, 1984), p. 37.
6. Whalen, *The Founding Father,* pp. 63–64.
7. Kennedy, *Times to Remember,* p. 80. See also Hamilton, *J.F.K.,* p. 41.
8. Kearns Goodwin, *The Fitzgeralds and the Kennedys,* p. 303 and p. 307.
9. Reeves, *A Question of Character,* p. 29.
10. Kearns Goodwin, *The Fitzgeralds and the Kennedys,* pp. 309–310. See also Hamilton, *J.F.K.,* p. 42.
11. Hamilton, *J.F.K.,* p. 43.
12. Collier and Horowitz, *The Kennedys,* pp. 58–59.
13. Reeves, *A Question of Character,* pp. 41–42.
14. Ibid., p. 44.
15. Ralph G. Martin, *A Hero for Our Time: An Intimate Story of the Kennedy Years* (New York, 1983), p. 25 and p. 31. See also Reeves, *A Question of Character,* p. 45.
16. Martin, *A Hero for Our Time,* p. 31.
17. Ibid.; and Hamilton, *J.F.K.,* p. 166.
18. Martin, *A Hero for Our Time,* p. 32.
19. Reeves, *A Question of Character,* p. 47.
20. Martin, *A Hero for Our Time,* p. 33.
21. Richard B. Morris and Graham W. Irwin, eds., *Harper Encyclopedia of the Modern World* (New York, 1970), pp. 419–420.
22. Hamilton, *J.F.K.,* p. 108.
23. Ibid., p. 224.
24. Collier and Horowitz, *The Kennedys,* pp. 96–97.
25. Joan and Clay Blair, Jr., *The Search for J.F.K.* (New York, 1976), pp. 80–81.
26. Arthur Krock, *Memoirs: Sixty Years on the Firing Line* (New York, 1968), p. 350. See also Hamilton, *J.F.K.,* p. 154.
27. Reeves, *A Question of Character,* pp. 49–50.
28. Ibid.

2

YEARS OF WAR

"For a long time, I was Joseph
Kennedy's son, then I was Joe's
brother. . . . Someday I hope to be able

to stand on my own feet."

fter he graduated from Harvard, John F. Kennedy
briefly thought about going to law school. His brother
Joe Jr. had enrolled at Harvard Law School, and Jack,
hoping finally to escape the long shadow of his older brother,
considered going to Yale. But once again bad health intervened
and, after he suffered a bout with ulcers, his doctors advised
Jack to take a year off to rest up.

In the summer of 1940 Jack traveled to California in search
of sun, young women and relaxation. While there he enrolled
at Stanford University in the School of Business Administration. Once again his health faltered, however, and by December, after only three months at Stanford, Jack Kennedy was
back in Boston and in the hospital. He spent much of the
remaining winter relaxing in Charlotte, North Carolina, Nas-
sau and Palm Beach. By the spring of 1941 he was once again
off vacationing, this time in South America, where he became
involved with two lovely young women who were the daughters
of a well-known Argentine diplomat.[1]

With war raging in Europe it looked as though it was only a
matter of time before the United States would be drawn into
the conflict. As college graduates began dealing with the
country's first peacetime draft following President Roosevelt's
declaration of "a state of national emergency," the Kennedy
brothers faced up to their military obligations. Joe Jr. joined

The Kennedy family of Massachusetts on the eve of World War II (John F. Kennedy Library)

the Naval Aviation Cadet Program at Harvard. "Wouldn't you know," his father complained, "naval aviation, the most dangerous thing there is."[2]

Some historians claim that Jack was rejected by both the army and the navy because of his weak back.[3] However, there is no evidence of this. Later, some distinguished historians and biographers were told that Jack Kennedy finally got into the navy as a result of "five months of strengthening exercises" for his troubled back. His mother Rose told a similar story for many years. The truth is that Ambassador Kennedy once again used his vast influence to see that his second son was able to join the navy. Ambassador Kennedy was able to pull some strings with his military contacts in Washington.

In August of 1941, without a single day of training, Jack Kennedy somehow passed his physical examination, and in September he was commisioned as an officer in the Naval Reserve with the rank of ensign. As two historians who investigated this aspect of Kennedy's life concluded, "A young man who could certainly not have qualified for the Sea Scouts on his physical condition, entered the U.S. Navy."[4]

His first assignment was a plum—a desk job in the Office of Naval Intelligence in Washington, D.C. Captain Alan Goodrich Kirk, a naval intelligence officer who had been the naval attache in London when Joseph Kennedy was ambassador, had been appointed director of the Office of Naval Intelligence (ONI). On August 8, 1941, he wrote Ambassador Kennedy, "About Jack, I shall hope to hear that his plans are progressing favorably and I will see that he gets an interesting job."[5]

On December 7, 1941, the Japanese attacked the United States at Pearl Harbor, and immediately Jack Kennedy itched to get into the thick of the fight. He had become romantically involved with a beautiful Danish journalist, Inga Arvad, who was said to have caught the eye of Adolf Hitler during the Berlin Olympic games of 1936. Because of Arvad's notorious Nazi contacts, some in Washington suspected that she was a German spy. The powerful director of the Federal Bureau of Investigation, J. Edgar Hoover, saw to it that a number of intimate conversations between Jack and his Scandinavian girlfriend were secretly recorded.[6]

Soon, Jack Kennedy was expressing great anger to Inga that he had been transferred from Washington to seamanship school at Northwestern University and then to sea duty. Once again, his father's influence was to play a major role in his life. As Jack told a friend in Boston,

> You know what they tried to do? They tried to ship me to Panama. So then I called the old man and told him what I wanted, that I wanted to see action. And the next day, just like that, the very next day, I had orders sending me off to this PT outfit in the Pacific.[7]

At about the same time, Jack's brother Joe Jr. graduated from flight training school in Florida and received his navy wings as an ensign in the Naval Reserve. Joe had been a bit upset that Jack had gotten his commission first—and without really earning it. But now he had become a member of one of the most elite groups in the armed services. Ambassador Kennedy himself made the trip north from Palm Beach to Jacksonville to address the graduates and proudly pin on his eldest son the gold wings certifying him as a naval aviator.[8]

Meanwhile, Jack's poor health again caused him to be hospitalized, both in Charleston, South Carolina and in Boston. Jack was in constant pain during his training and often slept on a table instead of a bed. To compensate for the fact that he had not worked as hard as big brother Joe for his commission, Jack wanted very much to go overseas for hazardous PT boat duty.

PT (patrol torpedo) boats had been receiving a great deal of attention because of the daring exploits of their crews in the early months of the war against Japan in the Pacific. The small, highly maneuverable craft were very hazardous to operate. They were made of plywood and carried 3,000 gallons of gasoline for their engines. One accurate shot from the enemy could easily turn the little boats into raging infernos. Much of the PT publicity that was engaging Americans at the start of the war in the Pacific was an attempt to bolster sagging morale at home after the defeat the U.S. armed forces had suffered at the hands of the Japanese at Pearl Harbor. It was a romantic notion to imagine that a few brave American sailors on a tiny wooden boat would take on a Japanese battleship. As Kennedy said,

> I worked hard at it because I liked PTs. I think I liked PTs because they were small. I don't think I gave much thought to world conditions and things during the war.[9]

In the fall of 1942 Ambassador Kennedy arranged for Jack's Harvard friend Torby Macdonald to join his son for the last stage of his PT training in Rhode Island. Jack graduated in December and immediately sought overseas duty. However, because of his bad back Jack was forced to stay on in Rhode Island as an instructor. As one of his fellow trainees stated, "Actually, to tell the truth, he had no business being in the military service at all."[10]

By March of 1943 the young PT boat skipper found himself in the Pacific. Based in the Solomon Islands near Guadalcanal, Kennedy was given command of PT 109, an 80-foot boat that had seen a great deal of action. Even though his men knew that he was the rich son of a famous father, the young commander was well liked and very much respected by the sailors who served under him.

On the dark and misty night of August 1, 1943, PT 109 was rammed by a Japanese destroyer. With his boat cut in half and two crewmen dead, Kennedy gave the order to abandon ship. Kennedy bravely aided one of his crewmen who was badly burned to swim back to the bow of their foundering PT boat after the fire subsided. Once there they clung to the wreckage throughout the long night.

The next morning, with the remains of PT 109 sinking, Kennedy and his crew began to swim toward Plum Pudding Island, a nearby atoll over three miles away. Kennedy courageously towed his severely burned crewman, Patrick Mac-Mahon, for four hours through dangerous waters holding a strap from the wounded man's lifejacket in his teeth. Kennedy's efforts were nothing less than heroic—especially when one considers his own poor physical condition at the time. Kennedy unquestionably saved his crewman's life.

Once they had made it to the deserted atoll, Kennedy warned his men to hide on the approach of any airplanes. Thus, inadvertently, the crew avoided the friendly aircraft that were searching for them. Then Kennedy made the foolish decision to swim out again into the dangerous currents and shark-infested waters to look for a passing PT boat that he could alert to his crew's plight. In his fatigued state Kennedy might easily have drowned making the two- to three-mile swim. On his way back, after failing to find a PT search and rescue mission, Kennedy was so tired he almost did drown. He made it back to the atoll by dawn, sick and feverish.[11]

Eventually Kennedy and his men were rescued. Meanwhile, his father put the family's powerful public relations machine into full gear. The point was to get the story out as quickly as possible to an American public that hungered to hear anything of a positive nature regarding the war in the Pacific. A story about a genuine war hero was just what the public needed—especially if that hero happened to be the son of Ambassador Joseph P. Kennedy. It wasn't very long before John F. Kennedy's heroic exploits with PT 109 became front-page news in many American newspapers and even began appearing in movie newsreels.

The famous writer John Hersey wrote a piece about Kennedy's exploits in the Pacific for *The New Yorker,* thus guaranteeing that Kennedy's heroism would not go unnoticed and would also someday become the stuff of legend. Ambassador Kennedy advanced the mythology by seeing to it that the *Reader's Digest* reprinted a condensed version of the Hersey article, and eventually hundreds of thousands of reprints, used to further John F. Kennedy's political career, found their way into the hands of the American public.

What is the truth about the PT 109 episode? It first alerted the American people to the presence in their midst of a dashing and heroic young navy officer who risked life and limb to save his men and who exercised leadership skills in the face of a harrowing, unexpected wartime disaster. No one could possibly deny that Jack Kennedy performed bravely and courageously in combat. However, many young Americans exhibited amazing courage against impossible odds during the course of World War II, and their stories hardly made it into the footnotes of the official military histories. As one historian has recently written,

> The perpetual inflation of the PT 109 story for political purposes reveals a basic lack of integrity on Jack's part. The facts of the matter reveal a very young man in bad physical condition to begin with, who performed poorly on his PT boat and exhibited some recklessness and poor judgment in the subsequent rescue efforts. Still, Kennedy displayed genuine courage after the crash and a willingness to do all in his power to save his men. The bravery was real, however it was exaggerated in campaign literature and in authorized books.[12]

When he became president of the United States, Kennedy privately admitted to close friends that much too much had been made of his wartime heroism and the PT 109 episode. (By then, however, it was too late. The mythology was solidified when Hollywood producers sank their teeth into a mediocre film of Kennedy's wartime exploits in the 1963 movie *PT-109*, starring Cliff Robertson as the young Jack Kennedy.) As Robert J. Donovan, the author of the best book on Kennedy's military service, observed in 1961, "It is even possible that he might never have reached the White House if it had not been for PT 109."[13]

John F. Kennedy returned to the United States for a two-week leave in January 1944. He was transferred to a PT unit in Miami with minimal duties, where most of the officers spent their time having fun and pursuing young women. However, his Pacific service had aggravated his bad back, and by June Kennedy was once again in the hospital. In mid-June he underwent unsuccessful disk surgery that left a gaping hole in his back. His back problems would pain and trouble him for the remainder of his life.

That summer, as he recuperated in Arizona, Jack spent hours each day talking to his father. Two family tragedies brought father and son closer together in those months and would, ultimately, launch John F. Kennedy's life in politics.

The first was close to home and devastated the Kennedy family: eldest son Joseph P. Kennedy, Jr. was killed on a mission when the experimental bomber he was flying was lost in a massive explosion over England. The news came to the Kennedy family on a warm day in mid-August of 1944 in Hyannis Port as they finished lunch at the family compound. Two priests arrived and asked Mrs. Kennedy to awaken her husband, who was taking a nap. Mrs. Kennedy later recalled,

> I ran upstairs and awakened Joe. I stood for a few moments with my mind half paralyzed. I tried to speak but stumbled over the words. Then I managed to blurt out that priests were here with that message. . . .We sat with the priests in a smaller room off the living room, and from what they told us we realized there could be no hope, and that our son was dead.[14]

The ambassador was grief-stricken. He was never again able to mention his eldest son's name without weeping. As his friend Arthur Krock of the *New York Times* remembered,

> The death of Joe, Jr. was the first break in this circle of nine children, nearly all extraordinary in some way: handsome, intelligent, with a mother and father to whom they were devoted and who were devoted to them. It was one of the most severe shocks to the father that I've ever seen registered on a human being.[15]

Later that summer, on September 10, Kathleen "Kick" Kennedy's English husband, Billy Hartigan, was killed in combat in Belgium. "We could scarcely believe it," Rose Kennedy said of her second daughter's loss. "It seemed too cruel that another tragedy had so soon befallen us."[16]

Like the other members of his family, John F. Kennedy was crestfallen over the death of his older brother. He had been at home on leave when the news of his brother's death arrived. Writing to a friend, he said,

> Joe's loss has been a great shock to us all. He did everything well and with great enthusiasm, and even in a family as large as ours, his place can't ever be filled.[17]

That fall Kennedy spent his time as an outpatient at the Chelsea Naval Hospital near Boston. He rested and exercised his aching back while collecting eulogies for a small book called *As We Remember Joe* that memorialized his late brother. The family had the book printed privately. That Christmas, while the family was vacationing at Palm Beach, his father made it clear to Jack that he was to take Joe's place in the Kennedy family. He was chosen to enter politics. "It was like being drafted," Kennedy said. "My father wanted his oldest son in politics."[18]

At first he resisted his father's wishes. Nobody knew better than Jack Kennedy himself that his poor health, lack of experience, basic shyness around strangers, and reputation as a sometime playboy would hardly be conducive to a successful career in American politics. Kennedy served a brief stint as a special correspondent for the influential Hearst newspaper chain, covering the British elections, the Potsdam Peace Conference and the founding of the United Nations. But eventually John F. Kennedy acceded to his father's powerful political ambitions for his sons: he finally decided to run for Congress in Boston. As Rose Kennedy wrote,

> It is true that the role he chose probably would have been different, and would have come later, had it not been for Joe Jr.'s death. Joe Jr. would have made a career in elective public office.[19]

However, one of Kennedy's closest political aides disagrees with that analysis. Writing shortly after Kennedy's death, Theodore C. Sorensen noted that after Joe's death, he entered the political arena—not to take Joe's place, as is often alleged, not to compete subconsciously with him, but as an expression of his own ideals and interests in an arena thereby opened to him.

Sorensen was convinced that Kennedy's initial entrance onto the stage of the American political arena "was neither involuntary nor illogical." As John F. Kennedy himself said, "Everything seemed to point to it in 1946." Politics was, after all, part of a long tradition that had been handed down on both sides of the family, going back to both grandfathers.[20]

Clearly, with the death of his brother, John F. Kennedy was under intense pressure. The competitive contest with brother Joe was now gone forever in his life. Jack had confided to Lem Billings that "his competition with his brother had defined his own identity." Joe Jr. had always been the focus in the Kennedy family for their father's fierce ambitions for his sons. In a special sense, Joe's presence had helped deflect those ambitions and allow the younger Kennedy boys to avoid the heavy responsibility of living up to their father's strong demands.

Now, with Joe Jr. gone, those ambitions had been rechanneled and now centered on Jack as the second eldest son. Ambassador Kennedy revealed his hopes for Jack when he wrote to an English friend on August 22, 1945: "Jack arrived home and is very thin, but he is becoming quite active in the political life of Massachusetts. It wouldn't surprise me to see him go into public life to take Joe's place."[21]

With the terrible trauma of his brother's loss behind him, John Fitzgerald Kennedy now embarked on the second phase of his life: a career in American politics. It was to be a journey that would take him all the way from the streets of Boston's ethnically diverse neighborhoods to the most powerful office in the modern world: the presidency of the United States.

Notes

1. Thomas C. Reeves, *A Question of Character: A Life of John F. Kennedy* (New York, 1991), p. 54.
2. Ibid., p. 55; and quoted in Doris Kearns Goodwin, *The Fitzgeralds and the Kennedys: An American Saga* (New York, 1987), p. 622.

3. David Burner, *John F. Kennedy and a New Generation* (Boston, 1988), p. 18. See also Joan and Clay Blair, Jr., *The Search for J.F.K.* (New York, 1976). The Blairs correct the myth that JFK's back problems stemmed from a Harvard football injury. They cite Dr. Elmer C. Bartels of the Lahey Clinic, where Kennedy had been treated for some unnamed illness. Dr. Bartels said that Kennedy was "born with an unstable back." He went on to explain: "An unstable back is something you are born with and it doesn't maintain itself properly." An unstable back is a problem that lasts throughout a patient's life. pp. 24–25.

4. Reeves, *A Question of Character,* p. 55; and quoted in Joan and Clay Blair, Jr., *The Search for J.F.K.,* p. 114.

5. Blair and Blair, *The Search for J.F.K.,* p. 114.

6. Burner, *John F. Kennedy and a New Generation,* p. 18.

7. Ralph G. Martin, *A Hero for Our Time: An Intimate Story of the Kennedy Years* (New York, 1983), p. 38.

8. Reeves, *A Question of Character,* p. 58.

9. Martin, *A Hero for Our Time,* p. 38.

10. Blair and Blair, *The Search for J.F.K.,* p. 166.

11. Reeves, *A Question of Character,* pp. 64–65.

12. Ibid., pp. 67–68.

13. Robert J. Donovan, *PT-109: John F. Kennedy in World War II* (New York, 1967), p. 155. See Donovan for the full and complete story of the PT 109 episode.

14. Rose Fitzgerald Kennedy, *Times to Remember* (New York, 1974), p. 301.

15. Arthur Krock, *Memoirs: Sixty Years on the Firing Line* (New York, 1968), p. 348.

16. Kennedy, *Times to Remember,* p. 301.

17. Theodore C. Sorensen, *Kennedy* (New York, 1965), p. 34.

18. Reeves, *A Question of Character,* p. 73.

19. Kennedy, *Times to Remember,* p. 305.

20. Sorensen, *Kennedy,* p. 15.

21. Kearns Goodwin, *The Fitzgeralds and the Kennedys,* p. 698 and pp. 705–706.

3

FROM THE HOUSE TO
THE SENATE

"I can't wait. I don't have time. I've got
to do it now."

Billy Sutton got out of the army in early 1946. He was still wearing his dress uniform when he took the train to Boston from nearby Fort Devens, where he had just been mustered out of the the service. Sutton was walking along School Street in downtown Boston when he ran into his old pal Joe Kane. Joe Kane was one of the Kennedy family's many cousins. Kane immediately enlisted the young soldier into the ranks of the Kennedys' growing political army. Sutton recalls:

> We walk around the corner to 21 Beacon St., the old Bellvue Hotel, and we go up to Room 308 and I meet Kennedy at the door. He was tall and gaunt. He asks me what I think of his fight. I tell him between Fitz (Honey Fitz, Kennedy's grandfather—the ex-mayor of Boston) and his father, he had a pretty good shot. And World War II was the best campaign manager you could have, if you were a veteran.

Sutton still remembers that historic day in his life. Almost fifty years later, he grins wickedly, saying, "And, you know, he had some cash."[1]

John F. Kennedy was *from* Boston. But he was hardly *of* it. He needed those young Irishmen who had grown up in the city's streets and who knew the neighborhoods. If anything, Boston is a city made up of neighborhoods, and every politician since

Kennedy has ignored the competitive ethnic turf of Boston at his or her dire peril.

Kennedy immediately liked Billy Sutton. He asked him if he had a job waiting for him after the army. When Sutton told Kennedy that he had a job waiting at Boston Consolidated Gas, Kennedy responded, "How about coming to work for me?" Within a few days Billy Sutton, out of his army uniform and wearing a brand-new suit, was working for the congressional campaign of John F. Kennedy. Sutton says,

> Everybody talks about Joe Kennedy, the father. He had the money. But he really didn't know the politics of Boston. He needed the Joe Kanes, the Patsy Mulkerns, the Mark Daltons, the Joe Healys.[2]

The Kennedys also needed Dave Powers. Powers, who went from the Boston neighborhood of Charlestown to Capitol Hill and all the way to the White House with John F. Kennedy, remembers their first campaign for Congress vividly.

When Kennedy scouted around the provincial wards and precincts of the 11th District in Boston for help in his first run for political office, Billy Sutton advised his new boss "to get Dave Powers in Charlestown because Dave knew every voter in Charlestown by his first name."

Dave Powers was a "townie" who had grown up in Boston selling newspapers at the Charlestown Navy Yard. He ushered at Saint Catherine's Church every week and coached the local Catholic Youth Organization teams. To get the politically savvy Powers on board would give Kennedy an instant jump-start on 10,000 needed voters.

So, on January 21, 1946, Jack Kennedy found himself climbing three flights of stairs to the top floor of the three-decker where Dave Powers lived with his widowed sister and her eight children. Years later, when Powers served as President Kennedy's special assistant in the White House, the president would often tease him, saying, "If I had gotten tired that night when I reached the second floor, I would never have met you."[3]

John F. Kennedy was obviously totally unfamiliar with the many three-deckers that dotted the Charlestown landscape, because he knocked on the front door on that freezing night. Anyone familiar with Charlestown residents in the cold Boston winters knew that most of the families who lived in the cold water flats of those endless three-deckers could be found gathered around the warmth of the stoves in their cozy kitchens in the back of the house.

As Dave Powers recalled Kennedy standing in the dim light of the hallway in his sister's apartment that winter's night,

> I could barely make out this tall and thin, handsome young fellow standing there alone in the darkness. . . . He stuck out his hand and said, 'My name is Jack Kennedy. I'm a candidate for Congress.' I said, 'Well, come on in.'[4]

Powers listened carefully to what Kennedy said. Finally, even though Powers had already committed to supporting another local candidate, he agreed to accompany the determined young Kennedy to a meeting of Gold Star Mothers (mothers who had lost their children in the war) at the American Legion hall in Charlestown. There could be little harm, he thought, in just going to a meeting.

According to those who knew him well, Kennedy was still a bit shy and awkward around strangers. He did not immediately take to the glad-handing and back-slapping that are so typical of Boston's ethnic politics. In fact, unlike most politicians of that era, Kennedy could not even be convinced to wear a hat that he could use to wave at the crowd. Sometimes he would be seen carrying a hat in his hand. Kennedy hated hats and even refused to wear them when he became president.

Kennedy also disliked the pretentiousness of arriving at a speaking date in a big limousine, surrounded by a crowd of his political advisers. So Kennedy and Powers hopped the subway to Charlestown to meet with the Gold Star Mothers. As Kennedy got up to speak, Powers couldn't help but think to himself, "This guy looks awfully young to be running for Congress."[5]

Kennedy spoke briefly and earnestly to the gathered women about the need to keep the world at peace, and on the sacrifices of war. He tugged at their emotions when he said, with some hesitation in his voice, "I think I know how all you mothers feel because my mother is a gold star mother, too." The women rushed up to meet the young candidate. He had touched them where they lived and he touched their hearts. Powers remembered,

I heard those women saying to each other, 'Isn't he a wonderful boy, he reminds me so much of my own John, or my Bob.' They all had stars in their eyes. It took him a half hour to pull himself away from them. They didn't want him to leave. I said to myself, I don't know what this guy's got. He's no great orator and he doesn't say much, but they certainly go crazy over him.[6]

Powers immediately enlisted in the Kennedy cause. He became Kennedy's man in Charlestown. He rented a store on Main Street for $50 a month as the campaign's local headquarters.

And so the real hard work of a Boston political campaign began. Powers's job was to round up his friends in the neighborhood who would come down to headquarters to make phone calls, stuff envelopes or do any of the other numberless little tasks needed to get a candidate known to the uninvolved voters of Boston. He arranged the afternoon teas, the evening coffee klatches, the street-corner rallies—anything it took to get his candidate out front to meet the thousands of voters who would be needed to elect him to office.

There were 17 candidates for the congressional seat of the outgoing congressman from the 11th District, the legendary Boston politician James Michael Curley. Kennedy's first task was to distinguish himself in such a large field. By early February Kennedy was working the streets of the district on a full-time basis. Billy Sutton recalled that for four months his boss got no more than four and a half hours of sleep a night. It was initially very difficult for the inexperienced young millionaire to go one-on-one with voters in the very personal style that has always characterized a rough-and-tumble Boston political campaign. One Kennedy adviser said,

He was very retiring. You had to lead him by the hand. You had to push him into the poolrooms, taverns, clubs, and organizations. He didn't like it at first. He wanted no part of it.[7]

Former speaker of the House of Representatives Thomas P. "Tip" O'Neill really got to know John F. Kennedy during that hectic first campaign. Recalling Kennedy's first congressional race, he says,

John F. Kennedy campaigns for Congress in 1946. (John F. Kennedy Library)

Jack played the game of politics by his own rules, which is why fellow politicians were so slow to take him seriously. During his early years in public life he hated shaking hands. . . . He hated crowds. When we went into a hall together, he'd immediately look for the back door. It was said that Jack Kennedy was the only pol in Boston who never went to a wake unless he had known the deceased personally.[8]

The Kennedy campaign strategy was simple and has worked well for countless Boston politicians ever since. He made sure that each neighborhood in the 11th District was covered by a local "Kennedy man." For Somerville he got Timothy J. Reardon; Mark Dalton and Francis X. Morrissey handled Boston; Tom Broderick organized Brighton; Billy Kelly was in East Boston; and John Droney had Cambridge. These tough-minded political operatives knew the local streets. Each was responsible for organizing in their territories; and each was, despite the multiethnic flavor of the 11th District, Irish. By the end of the election each of these men had recruited dozens of volunteers to the Kennedy campaign.

Many wondered whether the skinny kid who only had old Joe Kennedy's money behind him was up to the difficult task of a down-and-dirty Boston political race. One day when Francis X. Morrissey, who had headed the Community Fund in Boston, drove Kennedy to Maverick Square in the tough Italian section of East Boston, Morrissey wondered whether the young candidate could possibly deal with the stern-looking Sicilians who had gathered in the square. Kennedy completely disarmed them. As one writer described it,

> Morrissey watched while Kennedy went up to each of these characters, stuck out his hand, extracted a handshake, and soon had them talking and even smiling. Kennedy, Morrissey decided, would make out fine.[9]

The historian Henry Adams, great-grandson of President John Adams and grandson of President John Quincy Adams, felt that politics in Massachusetts was an exceedingly brutal game. As he observed, "Politics, as a practice, whatever its professions, had always been the systematic organization of hatreds, and Massachusetts politics had been as harsh as the climate."[10]

John F. Kennedy's first political campaign, however, did not live up to the Adams dictum. Instead of attacking the large field of candidates, Kennedy concentrated his efforts on reaching the voters in the district with a message that spoke directly to their needs, hopes and dreams. He talked about jobs, housing, medical care, veterans' benefits, Social Security and other matters that directly affected their pocketbooks.

Although the Kennedy campaign had plenty of money available for purchasing radio and newspaper ads, the real strength of John F. Kennedy as a candidate lay in his ability to meet and greet the voters and to touch them in a very personal sense.

With more than 100 volunteers, the Kennedy campaign set up house parties where Kennedy would have tea and cookies with a dozen or so voters at a time. In a single evening Kennedy's staff would schedule him to attend at least a half-dozen house parties.

At these parties, after overcoming his initial discomfort and shyness, Kennedy would flash his perfect trademark smile as he charmed both younger and older voters. Although house parties were hardly a new Boston political tradition, Kennedy was able to utilize the parlor meetings to their maximum potential as he endeared himself to many skeptical Boston voters, who typically distrusted most politicians.

Often, he would be accompanied by his mother and sisters. They would tell the voters what a wonderful son and brother Kennedy had been. Sometimes the family would converge at a large hotel in the district, where voters would be invited to meet the Kennedys. Rose Kennedy recalled one such night at the Hotel Commander in Cambridge:

> What happened was that fifteen hundred people came to the reception. At times the line stretched all the way through the hotel lobby, through the entranceway, and outside and far down the block. For all of them there were handshakes, smiles, and some words from each of us. There were a few men there, but most were women, all of whom seemed to have had their hair done for the event. Jack was marvelous with them.[11]

Even little brother Teddy, age 14, got into the process by running errands for the campaign. And it certainly didn't hurt when hundreds of reprints of the *Reader's Digest* condensed version of Kennedy's PT 109 exploits somehow found their way onto a Boston bus or subway seat.[12]

That June, Kennedy amassed a total of 22,183 votes in the primary—enough by far to win the election in a crowded field of 10 candidates (some of whom, it was rumored, were induced to enter the campaign under the direction of Kennedy's father to siphon away votes from other candidates).

Kennedy was so confident on election day that he went to see the Marx Brothers film *A Night in Casablanca* before the returns came in. At the election night celebration, Grandpa Honey Fitz hopped on a table to dance an Irish jig and sang his trademark song, "Sweet Adeline."

With 42% of the vote in the primary field, Kennedy didn't need to worry very much about the general election coming up that November. Even though the Republicans fielded a candidate to oppose Kennedy, the 11th District had not gone Republican in many years. In November, without campaigning very hard, John F. Kennedy beat his Republican opponent by more than two to one. He was on his way to Washington as a United States congressman with a safe seat from which he could launch himself as a nationally known political figure.[13]

Kennedy's arrival in Washington, D.C. with the freshman congressional class of 1947—a class that included a young California congressman named Richard M. Nixon—was hardly an occasion for national notice. And initially Kennedy did not do very much to distinguish himself from the pack.

In his first newsletter, Congressman Kennedy complained to his constituents about the lack of decent acoustics and the poor lighting in the House Chamber. He disliked the rudeness of his senior colleagues, who, Kennedy complained, often talked or read the newspaper during speeches by other congressmen.

Kennedy tried to maintain an air of independence from the rest of the delegation. He was alone among his Massachusetts fellow congressmen in his refusal to sign a request to pardon the legendary and roguish ex-mayor, ex-congressman and ex-governor of Massachusetts, James Michael Curley. Curley had been convicted of corruption and was serving time in prison. Kennedy's admirers have interpreted this decision as an early profile in Kennedy political courage.[14]

Even Kennedy's staff urged him to sign the petition for Curley's pardon. And his father argued that Curley had paved the way for Kennedy's election by vacating the congressional seat that Kennedy now held. But Kennedy's steadfast refusal to sign a pardon for the fading Boston politician may have had a lot more to do with revenge for what Curley had once done to Kennedy's beloved grandfather, Honey Fitz. As Curley's biographer Jack Beatty has pointed out, "'Don't get mad, get even,' would be Kennedy's motto in politics as it had been Curley's."[15]

Although Kennedy seemed to delight in interrogating witnesses on the Labor and Education Committee—one of the few aspects of the tedious work of Congress that he enjoyed— the House of Representatives was not the place for a young man with John F. Kennedy's burning ambitions. Tip O'Neill has written,

> In the House of Representatives, Jack had been a fish out of water. He didn't get along with leadership, and they resented his frequent absences and his political independence. Jack was never one to do his homework. He preferred to travel, and he was always being invited to speak around the state. . . . In all my years in public life, I've never seen a congressman get so much press while doing so little work.
>
> He didn't pay much attention to the public-service part of the job.[16]

If Kennedy disliked the nuts and bolts of congressional life, he adapted easily to the social side of the back-and-forth activities of a Washington politician. He maintained a three-room apartment on Bowdoin Street in Boston near the State House, keeping it for the rest of his life as his legal address.

In Washington, Kennedy rented a three-story town house in Georgetown, sharing it with his 24-year-old sister Eunice, along with Billy Sutton, a family cook, and a black valet. The Kennedys quickly became known for their posh Washington parties. The D.C. social and political set enjoyed playing parlor games with young congressmen like Richard Nixon and Wisconsin's Joseph McCarthy.

Kennedy's Boston congressional office was run by Frank Morrissey, who served as a watchdog, reporting on Jack's political and social activities to the ambassador. According to one historian, Joe Kennedy even placed a maid in his son's Georgetown home to report back to him.[17]

Congressman Kennedy did not come to Washington with a unique set of political beliefs. In fact, like many political leaders of the period that became known as the cold war era (when Russia and the United States, the two global superpowers, competed with one another on a worldwide basis), Kennedy's worldview was typical of the time in which he lived. He could hardly be characterized as an innovative or original thinker.

Kennedy followed his father and his church in the way he saw communism. In his eyes it was a worldwide menace that had to be stopped at any cost. Thus, when it came to foreign policy, John F. Kennedy remained a cold warrior for his entire political career. He viewed the Soviets, as President Ronald Reagan later described them, as an "evil empire." His votes usually reflected his views.

Thus, in 1948 Kennedy voted for more defense spending instead of a tax cut. Curiously, he was growing apart from the more conservative internationalism that characterized his father. While Joseph Kennedy favored cutting taxes and reducing government defense spending, Congressman John F. Kennedy supported the expanding role of American foreign policy on the world scene.

Kennedy favored the Truman Doctrine, a policy that was designed to stop the growth of communism in Greece and Turkey. Similarly, Kennedy supported the Marshall Plan and the European Recovery Program, two plans that became the bulwark of American foreign policy. The aim was to put the war-ravaged and impoverished nations of Europe back on their economic feet after the disaster of World War II. By supporting these poor nations financially, the United States was also promoting democracy and helping to prevent the development and spread of communism.

On domestic issues, John F. Kennedy was difficult to pigeon-hole early in his political career. Although the myth-makers of the Democratic Party seek to portray Kennedy as a natural heir to the liberalism in American social policy that began with Franklin D. Roosevelt and the New Deal, his early votes in Congress showed that Kennedy was all over the political spectrum. For example, he voted against funding of hospital construction, federal funding of rural cooperatives, aid to the Navajo and Hopi Indians, and expenditures for public libraries in regions that did not have them. Most significantly, Kennedy voted against a bill that would have prohibited discrimination in employment.

However, Kennedy did not entirely stray from the his political fold. He supported a bill to extend Social Security benefits, a minimum wage bill, and legislation to provide medical care for the impoverished. Kennedy was primarily interested in issues like housing for returning veterans, and he strongly supported legislation that he thought would benefit his working-class constituents. Those positions enabled Kennedy to oppose the Taft-Hartley bill, which was widely viewed as antilabor. Yet, unlike many other Democratic political leaders, he did not develop a strong working relationship with American labor leaders. He saw many of these tough-talking men as corrupt racketeers. Those views remained with Kennedy for his entire political life.[18]

The truth was that Kennedy was restless. He was bored by life in the House of Representatives. And, once again, he was plagued by illness. In the late 1940s Kennedy was diagnosed with Addison's disease—an adrenal insufficiency that made him susceptible to many secondary infections. His doctors put him on an oral cortisone medication that probably saved his life. In addition, Kennedy had recurring infections from the hole in his back—a problem that would become life-threatening a few years later.[19]

As his attendance in the House of Representatives dropped off, political friends and foes alike began to wonder what it was that Jack Kennedy wanted. It was no secret that Congressman Kennedy was spending more time chasing pretty young women than he was on the House floor. As Tip O'Neill said, "he had more fancy young girls flying in from all over the country than anyone could count."[20]

Meanwhile, tragedy again struck the Kennedy family. Kathleen "Kick" Kennedy had tried living at home with her parents in 1946 but couldn't get along well with her mother and father. During Jack's first campaign the family kept her out of public view for fear of losing Catholic votes (Kick's late husband had been a Protestant). In 1947 she returned to England, where she began a serious relationship with a handsome English aristocrat, Peter Milton, Lord Fitzwilliam.

In 1948 the 28-year-old Kick broke the news during a visit to her parents that she planned to marry her English lover. The problem was that Fitzwilliam was a Protestant, and married to boot. Her mother, Rose, the most devout Catholic in the

Kennedy clan, wouldn't hear of her daughter marrying a divorced man. She threatened to banish Kick from the family and to have the ambassador cut off her allowance.

The spirited Kick angrily defied her mother and returned to England. Still, she desperately sought her father's blessing before her decision to marry was made public. So, when Joe Kennedy was scheduled to be in Paris for a Marshall Plan fact-finding mission, Kathleen planned a meeting between her father and her future husband. On May 13, 1948, Kathleen and Lord Fitzwilliam left London in an eight-seat plane. They planned to fly to Cannes for a few days before heading for Paris and the meeting with her father. The plane flew into a raging thunderstorm and, after pitching violently in the storm for about 20 minutes, crashed into the side of a mountain near the tiny French town of Privas, killing everyone on board.

That evening Ambassador Kennedy was informed of the crash by a *Boston Globe* reporter. He rushed to Privas, hoping against hope that somehow his daughter was alive. There, escorted to the local town hall by the French police, Ambassador Kennedy tearfully identified his eldest daughter's mangled body.

In Washington, Jack was at home listening to a recording of the Broadway musical *Finian's Rainbow* when his sister Eunice told him that Kathleen might have been killed. Kennedy called his office and asked Tim Reardon, his executive assistant, to check out the facts. When the news of Kathleen's death was verified, the song "How Are Things in Glocca Morra?" came on. The singer, Kennedy told Billy Sutton, had a sweet voice. Then he turned away and began to weep. The fun-loving Kathleen, so much like him, had been his favorite sister.

On May 20 Kathleen was buried in her first husband's family plot in the English countryside. One Englishman there recalled,

> I can still see the stricken face of old Joe Kennedy as he stood alone, unloved and despised, behind the coffin of his eldest daughter amid the hundreds of British friends who had adored her and now mourned her. On one of the many wreaths there was even a handwritten note from former British wartime prime minister Winston Churchill.[21]

Rose Kennedy, convinced that her daughter had gone to hell for her sins, did not attend the funeral. It took the Kennedys a long time to get over Kathleen's untimely death. As Ambassador Kennedy wrote to a friend in England, "The sudden death of young Joe and Kathleen within a period of three years has left a mark on me that I find very difficult to erase."[22]

No one grieved more than Jack Kennedy. "After Kathleen's death," Lem Billings remembered, "Jack had terrible problems falling asleep at night. Just as he started to close his eyes, he would be awakened by the image of Kathleen sitting up with him late at night talking about their parties and dates. He would try to close his eyes again, but he couldn't shake the image."[23]

For a time Kennedy tried to replace the closeness he had lost by having a long string of superficial relationships with a number of young women. In some ways, life became meaningless. As his friend Billings said,

> He just figured there was no sense in planning ahead anymore. The only thing that made sense, he decided, was to live for the moment, treating each day as if it were his last, demanding of life constant intensity, adventure and pleasure.[24]

Once again the Kennedys turned to politics to assuage the overwhelming grief that hovered over their lives. With his health somewhat improved by 1950, Kennedy began to look at the upcoming 1952 Senate race in Massachusetts. He told his friend Congressman Hale Boggs of Louisiana that he was bored with the House and that he wanted to run for the Senate. "You don't know the House well enough to be bored by it. You haven't been here long enough," Boggs replied.[25]

The Senate seat eyed by John F. Kennedy was held by the aristocratic Republican Henry Cabot Lodge, Jr., the grandson of the man who had beaten Kennedy's grandfather, Honey Fitz, in 1916. Lodge had occupied the seat securely since 1936, when he beat James Michael Curley by 142,000 votes. He was well liked, well financed, and close to the popular former general Dwight D. Eisenhower, who would eventually become the Republican Party's 1952 candidate for president of the United States.

Even though he was a Republican, Lodge had enjoyed a good relationship with the Kennedys over the years. In fact, in 1942 Joseph Kennedy had even contributed to Lodge's campaign against a candidate backed by then-President Franklin D. Roosevelt.[26]

However, Ambassador Kennedy managed to persuade his son to run against Lodge. "When you've beaten him, you've beaten the best. Why try for something less?" Joseph Kennedy said. As Arthur Krock wrote, "The move to the Senate was inevitable in the pursuit of the ambition that Kennedy's father conceived before the future President had."[27]

To prepare the way for his coming campaign, each week Congressman Kennedy would fly to Boston from Washington late Thursday night and spend the long three-day weekend on the campaign trail with a few selected aides. He kept a map of Massachusetts on the wall of his Bowdoin Street apartment and would put a colored pin in every city and town he visited.

By 1951 the map was fully covered with colored pins. Kennedy aide Frank Morrissey, who often accompanied the congressman, later said, "I'll bet he talked to at least a million people and shook hands with seven hundred and fifty thousand."

Morrissey may not have overstated the vast Kennedy effort. Kennedy visited each of the 39 Bay State cities more than once and almost every one of the 312 towns. Wherever he was invited—schools and colleges, factories, veterans' clubs, fishing villages, church communion breakfasts—Kennedy was a tireless campaigner with but a single purpose: to communicate with the voting public and to make the Kennedy name, along with the Kennedy record, known to the voters of his state.

Many of his friends worried that he was driving himself too hard and that his health would once again become a casualty of his ambition. His close friend George Smathers chided him for working too hard, and Kennedy responded characteristically: "I can't wait. I don't have time. I've got to do it now!" Obviously, Jack Kennedy didn't think he would live long enough to enjoy his old age.[28]

By April of 1952 Massachusetts Governor Paul Dever finally made it clear to the Kennedys that he was not going to challenge Lodge for the Senate. Lodge, the governor felt, would just be too tough to beat. Kennedy didn't waste any time. He immediately jumped into the breech and publicly announced his candidacy:

> There is not only a crisis abroad, but there is a crisis here at home in Massachusetts. . . . For entirely too long the representatives of Massachusetts in the United States Senate have stood by helplessly while our industries and jobs disappear. . . . I, therefore, am opposing Henry Cabot Lodge, Jr., for the office of United States Senator from Massachusetts.[29]

Once again Joseph Kennedy operated his son's political fortunes from behind the scenes. He put Jack's younger brother, Robert F. Kennedy, in overall charge of the campaign. It turned out to be a wise move, because nobody worked harder in the Senate race than Bobby. He was the first to arrive at headquarters every morning and the last to leave at night. Bobby said,

> We organized women. They'd leave leaflets on seats when they got off a bus, and toss them through the doors of taxicabs so that the next passenger would have something to read—nine hundred thousand copies of our folder— were distributed by hand. . . . We tried to telephone every voter in Massachusetts at least twice in that campaign.[30]

And once again, Joseph Kennedy's vast fortune came in handy. When the powerful *Boston Post* threatened to endorse Lodge, Joseph Kennedy saw to it that the publisher was given a $500,000 loan. As John F. Kennedy later told a friend, "You know we had to buy that [expletive deleted] paper, or I'd have been licked." As Joseph Kennedy reminded his son:

> It takes three things to win in politics. The first is money, the second is money, and the third is money.[31]

Among the obstacles Kennedy had to overcome was the fact that he was relatively unknown and that 1952 was a presidential election year. The popular World War II military hero General Dwight D. Eisenhower was the Republican candidate for president of the United States. His opponent, Governor Adlai E. Stevenson of Illinois, did not seem to have the stature to carry either Massachusetts or the nation, and a landslide for Eisenhower could easily have buried the political career of

John F. Kennedy. Stevenson was looked upon as an intellectual, and the fact that he was divorced disturbed many voters, especially in a Catholic state like Massachusetts.

On election day Eisenhower swamped Stevenson across the country, and won in Massachusetts by 208,800 votes. The Democratic governor, Paul Dever, was beaten by Christian Herter as the voters of Massachusetts moved into the Republican ranks. However, Kennedy beat Lodge 1,211,984 to 1,141,247—a margin of more than 70,000 votes.

What happened? How did John F. Kennedy defeat the veteran politician Henry Cabot Lodge and begin a career in the United States Senate that, though undistinguished, would take him to the White House?

Again, the Kennedy family and fortune came into play. In the weeks before the election, thousands of Massachusetts women found themselves formally invited to fancy hotels for a series of parties throughout the state. Usually hosted by Rose Kennedy and managed by sisters Eunice, Jean and Pat, the receptions featured face-to-face meetings between the women and the handsome candidate.

In the end many factors contributed to Kennedy's victory, and it would be unfair to claim that Kennedy simply bought the election out from under the noses of the otherwise victorious Republicans. As Kennedy biographer James MacGregor Burns has explained,

> Kennedy's money, his father's influence and mobilization
> of public-relations people, the tea parties, the Kennedy
> family, Lodge's inability to campaign during most of the
> year, the defection of the Taft men [Taft was the Republi-
> can senator from Ohio who had opposed Eisenhower].
> Certainly all these were factors.[32]

Kennedy's Senate victory was not won on the issues. Very little differentiated Kennedy from Lodge on matters of substance. The voters of Massachusetts instead chose style over substance. It all came down to personality, and Kennedy had indeed become a major personality. And no matter what voters thought about the crucial issues of the day, the Kennedys had great style. As the age of easy celebrity was about to dawn in the American media, John F. Kennedy was on the verge of bringing his celebrity onto the main stage of American politics.

Of course, the 1952 Senate race was fought out on a far broader political plain. Essentially, the battle was between the old-line Protestant Republicans and the immigrant Catholic Democrats of Massachusetts. John F. Kennedy had been able to hold the ethnic coalition together and bring down the powerful Yankees in Bay State politics. But the United States still had never had a Catholic president. And whether the Kennedy victory in Massachusetts, 36 years after his grandfather had been beaten politically by another Lodge, would have any national meaning still remained to be seen as Jack Kennedy entered the United States Senate in 1953.

Notes

1. *Boston Globe,* July 18, 1993, p. 57.
2. Ibid.
3. Kenneth P. O'Donnell and David F. Powers with Joe McCarthy, *"Johnny, We Hardly Knew Ye": Memories of John Fitzgerald Kennedy* (New York, 1973), p. 57.
4. Ibid., p. 58.
5. Quoted in O'Donnell and Powers with McCarthy, *"Johnny, We Hardly Knew Ye,"* pp. 59–60. See also James MacGregor Burns, *John Kennedy: A Political Profile* (New York, 1959), p. 57.
6. O'Donnell and Powers with McCarthy, *"Johnny, We Hardly Knew Ye,"* p. 60.
7. Thomas C. Reeves, *A Question of Character: A Life of John F. Kennedy* (New York, 1991), p. 79.
8. Thomas P. O'Neill with William Novak, *Man of the House* (New York, 1987), p. 85.
9. Burns, *John Kennedy,* p. 64.
10. Henry Adams, *The Education of Henry Adams* (New York, 1931), p. 7.
11. Burns, *John Kennedy,* pp. 66–67; and quoted in Rose Fitzgerald Kennedy, *Times to Remember* (New York, 1974), p. 319.
12. David Burner, *John F. Kennedy and a New Generation* (Boston, 1988), p. 22.

13. Burns, *John Kennedy,* pp. 68–69.
14. Ibid., pp. 92–93.
15. Burner, *John F. Kennedy and a New Generation,* p. 23; and quoted in Jack Beatty, *The Rascal King: The Life and Times of James Michael Curley (1874–1958)* (Reading, Massachusetts, 1992), p. 480.
16. O'Neill with Novak, *Man of the House,* p. 87.
17. Reeves, *A Question of Character,* pp. 85–87.
18. Burner, *John F. Kennedy and a New Generation,* pp. 23–25.
19. Ibid., p. 25.
20. O'Neill with Novak, *Man of the House,* p. 87.
21. Doris Kearns Goodwin, *The Fitzgeralds and the Kennedys: An American Saga* (New York, 1987), pp. 737–740.
22. Reeves, *A Question of Character,* p. 94.
23. Kearns Goodwin, *The Fitzgeralds and the Kennedys,* p. 744.
24. Ibid.
25. Ralph G. Martin, *A Hero for Our Time: An Intimate Story of the Kennedy Years* (New York, 1983), p. 50.
26. Peter Collier and David Horowitz, *The Kennedys: An American Drama* (New York, 1984), p. 183. See also Burner, *John F. Kennedy and a New Generation,* p. 102.
27. Martin, *A Hero for Our Time,* p. 50; and quoted in Arthur Krock, *Memoirs: Sixty Years on the Firing Line* (New York, 1968), p. 357.
28. Burns, *John Kennedy,* p. 100; O'Donnell and Powers with McCarthy, *"Johnny, We Hardly Knew Ye,"* p. 91; and quoted in Collier and Horowitz, *The Kennedys,* p. 178.
29. Burns, *John Kennedy,* p. 102.
30. Martin, *A Hero for Our Time,* p. 51.
31. Ibid.
32. Burns, *John Kennedy,* p. 115.

4

HEADING FOR THE WHITE HOUSE

"All right, let's go."

Even his admirers admit that John F. Kennedy's time in the United States Senate was undistinguished. As Kennedy's top aide and speechwriter, Theodore Sorensen, has written, "John Kennedy was not one of the Senate's great leaders. Few laws of national importance bear his name."[1]

The initial task before Kennedy was to give the impression of diligence in the Senate. Arthur Krock writes, "Once in the Senate, Jack Kennedy began studiously, industriously, and intelligently to cultivate in the national field the 'public image' that had attracted the voters of Massachusetts." Krock, however, bought into the well-crafted mythology put out by the Kennedy people that Jack Kennedy was working hard to master the practice of being a serious lawmaker. Krock believed, "He [Kennedy] specialized, and with enormous burning of the midnight oil, on issues of education, labor, and foreign policy."[2]

The reality was that, during his early senatorial career, Jack Kennedy still spent more time specializing in escorting and chasing beautiful young women than he did in studying the practice of government and legislation. Recognizing that fact, his father understood better than anyone that the first order of business for the new senator from Massachusetts would have very little to do with the art or process of good government.

In 1953 Senator Kennedy turned 36. It was time, his father told him, to settle down and get married. The ambassador saw a wife and a family as vital political assets for a budding political superstar. In the decade of the 1950s a politician could hardly become a national political commodity if the American public viewed him as an irresponsible, rich playboy.

In January of 1953 Senator Kennedy attended the gala Eisenhower inaugural ball with Jacqueline Bouvier, a beautiful and polished young woman who was working as a photo journalist in Washington. The couple had been introduced at a friend's dinner party the previous spring, and by the fall they were romantically linked by the gossip columnists. At first, Jacqueline Bouvier wasn't overly impressed with the young senator. She told her cousin, John H. Davis, that Kennedy was vain and ambitious. "Oh sure, he's ambitious all right," she laughingly told Davis, "he even told me he intends to be president some day."[3]

Jacqueline Lee Bouvier had studied at Vassar and the Sorbonne. She had seen much of Europe before she was out of her teens. A 1951 graduate of George Washington University, Jackie landed a job, with the help of Arthur Krock, at the *Washington Times-Herald.*

She was the daughter of a once-wealthy New York stockbroker, John Vernou Bouvier. In 1940 her father, nicknamed "Black Jack," was divorced by her mother Janet, who then married a wealthy, twice-divorced millionaire, Hugh D. Auchincloss. By the time Jacqueline was in her teens her father, a bit of a playboy in his own right, had squandered a small family fortune. Thus, even though she had been raised in the exclusive and aristocratic world of fine horses and fox hunts, country estates and debutante balls, Jacqueline Bouvier was a young woman with little money—her newspaper job paid $42.50 a week—and she stood to inherit very little from her stepfather, who had children of his own to worry about. Thus, in the heady whirl of Washington society in the early 1950s, Jacqueline Bouvier was searching for a wealthy husband to maintain the high standard of living to which she had become accustomed. When she made her social debut in Newport, Rhode Island, the well-known society gossip columnist "Cholly Knickerbocker" had dubbed Jackie "Queen Deb of the Year."[4]

Although she had been engaged to a young stockbroker, her mother actively discouraged the marriage because the young man, John G. W. Husted, Jr., was not sufficiently wealthy. After meeting Kennedy, Jackie distanced herself from Husted and finally returned his engagement ring. As her relationship with Kennedy intensified, Jackie was exposed to all the rumors about the dashing and handsome senator from Massachusetts. Even Lem Billings had warned Jackie about his friend's illnesses and his many love affairs.[5]

Jackie was apparently unfazed. Jacqueline Bouvier was a young woman who knew exactly what she wanted out of life. A few months after she dropped her fiancé, and shortly after the *Saturday Evening Post* published a major story entitled "The Senate's Gay Young Bachelor," the couple announced their engagement.

John White, a close friend of Jackie's, observed,

> I think for Jackie the desire to conquer JFK was first of all the money. . . . I don't think Jackie cared much about JFK's morals. . . . More important to her than his morality was that he be at the center of events and that he acquit himself well and give her a decent role in the drama. It's fair to say they both lived up to their ends of the bargain.[6]

It was not a very long engagement. On September 12, 1953, the Kennedy-Bouvier wedding at St. Mary's Church in posh Newport, Rhode Island was one of the most talked-about social events of the season, with an invited guest list of 700. The *New York Times* reported that more than 3,000 spectators gathered at the police barriers around the church that morning just to get a glimpse of the 36-year-old groom and his 24-year-old bride.

The service, a nuptial high mass, was conducted by Kennedy family friend and confidant Richard Cardinal Cushing, the archbishop of Boston. The one drawback of the storybook day was the fact, obvious to all who attended, that Jackie's father, although spotted that day drunk in Newport, did not attend the wedding. One of Jackie's many strengths was her ability to conceal her emotions in public. Later that day she wept—in private.

Her mother's husband, Hugh Auchincloss, filled in for Black Jack Bouvier and gave the bride away. After spending their wedding night in New York, the couple flew off to Mexico City on the first leg of their honeymoon in Mexico. In Acapulco, as a result of a contact made by Joseph Kennedy, they stayed at the villa of Don Miguel Aleman, the president of Mexico.[7]

On the surface the Kennedy marriage appeared magical—as if Prince Charming had married Snow White. It was supposed to look that way. In the world of the Kennedys the most important concept was image. The way things looked was always far more important than the way things really were. The reality was that the Kennedy marriage was not very happy. Over the years Jack would often leave his wife and go off on vacations with his old buddies. He was not even present when Jackie suffered the first of two miscarriages before the birth of Caroline in 1957 and John Jr. in 1960.

Jacqueline Kennedy would spend a great deal of her time by herself, and when her husband was around they were rarely alone together. She developed rather extravagant tastes, going on frequent shopping sprees. Her love for expensive clothes and her cavalier spending habits became a point of contention between the couple. Jack Kennedy, who rarely carried much cash in his pockets, was constantly borrowing from his friends and was known to be something of a cheapskate.

As the years passed it was no secret to her close friends that Jackie was an unhappily married woman. To make matters worse, her husband continued to have involvements with other women, and there was a whispered rumor that the only reason Jackie didn't leave the marriage was the fact that Joseph Kennedy gave her a million dollars to stay married to his son after he became president.[8]

Like his far-from-perfect storybook marriage, John F. Kennedy's senatorial career needed shoring up. Kennedy now began increasingly to move around the country as if he were running for something far beyond the United States Senate. Tip O'Neill said,

> I knew Jack was serious about running for president back in 1954, when he mentioned that he intended to vote for the St. Lawrence Seaway project. The whole Northeast delegation was opposed to that bill, because once you opened the seaway you killed the port of Boston, which was the closest port to Europe. . . . Although he acknowledged that the seaway would hurt Boston, he supported it because the project would benefit the country as a whole.[9]

Another historian notes, "He worked now as as if he were a senator from New England, not just Massachusetts."

Kennedy had to institute some serious damage control as he took his political show on the road. Many of Kennedy's earlier positions and statements were out of step with the liberal wing of the Democratic Party. Most notable had been his staunch anticommunist statements, made as a result of the strong influence of his father and of his father's close friend Joseph McCarthy, the Republican senator from Wisconsin. The Kennedy tie to McCarthy was so powerful that Robert Kennedy had even taken a job as one of the Wisconsin demagogue's top Senate staff investigators.

Kennedy's once-frequent flirtation with the anticommunist ravings of McCarthy all but ended as the Kennedy men did their best to put some distance between the rising political star of Senator Kennedy and the rapidly fading star of McCarthy. Kennedy appeared on national television news shows like NBC's "Meet the Press," declaring that the federal government was no longer filled with subversive communists, as Senator McCarthy had charged on many occasions after his famous Wheeling, West Virginia speech in 1950.

Kennedy even began to delve into American foreign policy. He came to understand that the strong impulse toward nationalism in Third World countries was far more than a simple struggle between the forces of communism and democracy. He saw that nationalism, the tendency toward pride in nationhood and the strong demand for self-government in emerging nations, was perhaps no different from what the new nation of the United States had experienced after the American Revolution. Kennedy even went so far as to condemn the French for their involvement in Indochina, and told a group in 1952 that the United States should not send troops to Vietnam.[10]

The facade of his home life and his hectic political schedule took a toll on Kennedy. Once again, his health began to deteriorate. His days were increasingly filled with pain as his spinal condition, aggravated by irregular hours and the poor diet that inevitably accompanies the tedious political rounds, grew progressively worse. By the summer of 1954 Kennedy was forced to use crutches in order to get around. Because of his wartime ordeal, the recurrent effect of malaria and fevers, and the onset of Addison's disease, Kennedy suffered from a serious adrenal deficiency that weakened his body's natural defenses against the onslaught of infection.

It was clear to his doctors that Kennedy needed an operation. A physician who was also a close friend told Kennedy that his chances for surviving such an operation would be slim. When she left, Kennedy punched his crutches, telling a friend, "I'd rather die than spend the rest of my life on these things."[11]

That October Kennedy entered Manhattan's Hospital for Special Surgery, where he underwent a double spinal disc fusion. Three days after the surgery, infection set in and Kennedy went into a coma. He was given the last rites of the Catholic Church, and the family prepared itself, for yet another tragedy. Ambassador Kennedy visited his old friend Arthur Krock and slumped into a chair, weeping. "He told me," Krock recalled, "he thought Jack was dying."[12]

The Kennedy family and his Senate staff did their best to cover up the real cause of the operation—the Addison's disease. Kennedy's private secretary, Evelyn Lincoln, received contradictory bulletins from the hospital. At one point Kennedy seemed to rally, and the next moment he seemed to sink closer to death. Meanwhile, the press went along with the Kennedy public relations efforts and cooperated in linking his ordeal to the injuries from his wartime heroics. This story, of course, deceived the public.

Finally, the crisis was over. Kennedy came around and slowly began to improve. He would remain in the hospital through late December, and the public word was that Kennedy was almost totally incapacitated. The truth was that, even though he was in severe pain, he was alert and conscious. Still, Kennedy managed to miss the crucial vote in the United States Senate to censure Senator Joseph McCarthy. Kennedy and his aides maintained that he was too ill to vote on December second. But Kennedy could easily have paired his vote with another senator's by simply contacting that senator. Kennedy's chief aide, Theodore Sorensen, tried to shoulder the blame himself, writing that

> The responsibility for recording or not recording him on the censure vote in November, 1954, thus fell on me. I knew, had he been present, that he would have voted for censure along with every other Democrat.[13]

However, this is somewhat misleading, because Sorensen later admitted that not only "was Kennedy sufficiently conscious in that hospital to get a message to me on how he wanted to be paired. I think he deliberately did not contact me."[14]

The censure vote against McCarthy passed by a large margin on December 12 in the Senate. But liberal Democrats like former first lady Eleanor Roosevelt never forgot the fact that Kennedy, for whatever reasons, backed away from playing a moral role in the political demise of the man who was largely responsible for the anticommunist hysteria that swept the country in the early 1950s. As Mrs. Roosevelt suggested in her memoirs,

> A public servant must clearly indicate that he understands the harm that McCarthyism did to our country and that he opposes it actively, so that one would feel sure that he would always do so in the future.[15]

Curiously, although Kennedy's political courage seemed to have failed him in the McCarthy censure episode, he used the months of his convalescence to gain a national reputation for himself with the publication of a book he titled *Profiles in Courage*.

Although Kennedy's life was no longer in jeopardy, even though he had to return to New York for a second serious operation in February 1955, his friends and aides worried about his mental state. They feared that after a prolonged period of pain, combined with the fact that he had been bedridden and inactive for months, Kennedy might become depressed.

Kennedy solved the problem himself in early 1954 when he had suggested to his aides that he had an idea for an article on courageous figures in American history who had defended unpopular positions.

The article, prepared after some recuperative hospital reading, with the aid of a research team that included Theodore Sorensen, Georgetown University history professor Jules Davids, and former Harvard University Law School dean James M. Landis, soon grew into a book. Published in 1956, *Profiles in Courage* became a best-seller, and the following year the book was awarded the prestigious Pulitzer Prize.[16]

An immediate controversy followed the book's publication: Who actually was the author?

In the book itself Kennedy didn't appear to hide the fact that he had a great deal of help in its preparation and writing. He wrote,

> The greatest debt is owed to my research associate, Theodore C. Sorensen, for his invaluable assistance in the assembly and preparation of the material upon which this book is based.[17]

Sorensen saw the book as "a tonic to his spirits and a distraction from his pain," and has always maintained that Kennedy "was clearly the author of *Profiles in Courage* with sole responsibility for its concept and contents," Sorensen even agreed to furnish a sworn statement that he was not the author of the book.[18]

However, in recent years historians have examined the original manuscript of the book, located in the Kennedy Library in Boston, and one major Kennedy scholar, Herbert Parmet, has concluded that the manuscript actually bears little resemblance to the finished book as it was published. Parmet describes the manuscript as a "disorganized, somewhat incoherent melange from secondary sources." To be fair, like many modern authors who seek the help of researchers or ghost writers, Kennedy most likely served as the book's editor, with ultimate responsibility for what was or was not included in the final text, even though Sorensen was responsible for the book's lively style and easy readability. There is still no final verdict on the book's authorship, but Professor James Mac-Gregor Burns, who also was listed by Kennedy as one of the book's many contributors, probably came closest to the truth when he wrote, "He [Kennedy] had more help in the preparation of *Profiles in Courage* than authors customarily have, because of his illness; nonetheless, he wrote his own book."[19]

The success of *Profiles in Courage*—the fact that it became a best-seller and won the Pulitzer Prize—propelled John F. Kennedy into the national consciousness. The media greeted Kennedy as a returning hero when he came back to Washington on May 23, 1955. Family and friends welcomed him at National Airport, and he received a standing ovation when he entered Room 362 in the Senate Office Building. There was even a large basket of fruit with a note that said "Welcome

Home," signed "Dick Nixon." (In 1953, Nixon, the Republican senator from California, had become vice president of the United States in the Eisenhower administration.)

Kennedy's national notoriety soon attracted eager political outsiders who wished to make their mark on the Washington establishment. The well-known Hollywood screenwriter and producer Dore Schary cast about the country for an attractive politician to narrate his campaign film, *The Pursuit of Happiness,* extolling the virtues of the Democratic Party. The film was slated to be shown at the 1956 Democratic convention in Chicago. Over lunch with Schary, the respected CBS broadcaster Edward R. Murrow suggested the rising senator from Massachusetts. Murrow described Kennedy as "young, bright, charismatic, and definitely on his way up."[20]

Meanwhile, Kennedy had his trusted aide Ted Sorensen analyze voting records from recent national elections. Sorensen delivered a detailed analysis that he leaked to the national press to show that a Catholic running mate would be a positive advantage to a Protestant candidate for the presidency on the Democratic ticket.

Kennedy had diligently courted the southern and largely non-Catholic wing of the Democratic Party. He went out of his way to make friends with a number of conservative southern Democrats like Congressman John Rankin of Mississippi and Senators Richard Russell of Georgia and George Smathers of Florida.

Since 1928, when Governor Al Smith of New York, a Catholic, had been defeated for the presidency, the question of whether or not a Catholic could be elected to the presidency had been hotly debated. Of course, the big difference between 1928 and 1956 was the very important fact that the Catholic population in the United States had substantially increased—especially in big cities and in states that had a large number of presidential electoral votes.[21]

Kennedy's narration of the Schary film was his first major step onto the national political stage. After the technicolor film was shown at the convention, Kennedy appeared on the rostrum, to the absolute delight of the cheering and placard-waving Massachusetts delegation. Many of the signs read "Kennedy for Vice President." For the first time in modern American political history, television was to play a major role in the American political drama of nominating and electing a president. And that night the lesson was not lost on Kennedy or on his supporters as John F. Kennedy became instantly known to tens of millions of Americans.

The next day the convention easily nominated Adlai E. Stevenson for the presidency for the second time. Stevenson shocked everyone when he declined to perform the traditional role of a candidate in choosing a running mate. He told the convention's delegates, "The choice will be yours. The profit will be the nation's."[22]

The following day Senator Estes Kefauver of Tennessee beat Kennedy on the third ballot for the vice-presidential nomination. Kennedy was deeply disappointed, and would hold his defeat against Stevenson for many years. Stevenson, Kennedy felt, had been weak and indecisive. Kennedy was described by his aides Dave Powers and Kenneth O'Donnell as "frustrated" and "furious." They wrote, "He hated to lose anything, and he glared at us when we tried to console him by telling him that he was the luckiest man in the world." Kennedy, not conditioned to losing, responded angrily:

> This morning all of you were telling me to get into this thing and now you're telling me I should feel happy because I lost it.[23]

Only Kennedy's father seemed happy with the results. Kept far away from the political action of the Democratic convention, the elder Kennedy knew that the Stevenson ticket was doomed to lose. "Stevenson can't take Eisenhower," Joseph Kennedy said. "Jack's better off without it. If he runs with Stevenson, they'll blame the loss on his being Catholic. Besides, if you're going to get licked, get licked trying for first place, not second. He's better off running for the top spot in '60."[24]

Ultimately, John F. Kennedy came to agree with his father. As he told Dave Powers after the Democratic convention,

> With only about four hours of work and a handful of supporters, I came within thirty-three and a half votes of winning the Vice-Presidential nomination. If I work hard for four years, I ought to be able to pick up all the marbles.[25]

From that point on through 1960, Kennedy concentrated his efforts on capturing the presidency in 1960. As Kennedy historian Doris Kearns Goodwin writes,

> From 1956 forward all his actions would be designed to fortify his drive for the presidency. The campaign itself would be constructed within the tacit limits imposed by the Eisenhower presidency: the General's immense personal popularity made it difficult to articulate the underlying discontent, the vaguely sensed stagnation.[26]

Beyond the fact that Kearns Goodwin seems to forget that Eisenhower was no longer a general—he was president of the United States—there has always been the notion that the decade of the 1950s was a placid and dull time in American history, an era, as Kearns Goodwin describes it, of "stagnation." One must recall that it was the fifties that gave the nation new musical forms like rock and roll, with exciting performers like Elvis Presley, and new styles of acting and filmmaking with, directors like Stanley Kubrick and Alfred Hitchcock, and talented actors like James Dean and Marlon Brando. Still the perception of the 1950s as an uneventful decade has persisted during the decades that followed the tumultuous 1960s. It has been all but lost on too many scholars and writers of later decades that although the 1950s were by and large peaceful years, they were by no means placid, dull or boring.

It must be remembered that John F. Kennedy, for better or worse, was a political prodigy of that peculiar decade. Over a 10-year span, helped especially by the growth of television and its vast availability to the American masses by 1960, Kennedy had become virtually a national political celebrity. By 1958, at least 100 invitations to speak came streaming into his office each week. Kennedy crisscrossed the nation, accepting as many speeches as he could. He spoke on the Middle East to the National Conference of Christians and Jews; on liberty to the American Jewish Committee; he spoke to the Arkansas Bar Association and at dozens of Democratic Party functions. In 1957 he gave at least 150 talks around the country, and in 1958 he gave 200 more.[27]

Before 1956, if Kennedy wanted to publish a few articles in popular magazines he would have to submit them like any other writer. After 1956, editors and publishers eagerly sought John F. Kennedy's byline. He published an article on his illness in the *American Weekly;* a piece on brotherhood in *Parade,* the popular Sunday supplement that appears in newspapers every week across the country; articles in the *Saturday Evening Post,* in the *New York Times Magazine* and other popular periodicals. But Kennedy wanted to be read far beyond the popular culture and media. Seeking the approval and support of the Democratic intellectual establishment, Kennedy also appeared with strategic frequency in scholarly and specialized periodicals like the *Foreign Policy Bulletin* and the *National Education Association Journal.*[28]

Finally, on January 20, 1960, John F. Kennedy called an important press conference in the Senate Caucus Room. Kennedy told the gathered reporters, "I am announcing today my candidacy for the presidency of the United States." Kennedy confidently noted that the United States was about to enter an exciting new era. With his leadership, this period would stand in stark contrast to the passivity of the Eisenhower years that would be continued in the unhappy event of the election of Richard M. Nixon.[29]

The last step of John F. Kennedy's long American political journey was about to begin.

Notes

1. Theodore C. Sorensen, *Kennedy* (New York, 1965), p. 43.
2. Arthur Krock, *Memoirs: Sixty Years on the Firing Line* (New York, 1968), p. 357.
3. Thomas C. Reeves, *A Question of Character: A Life of John F. Kennedy* (New York, 1991), p. 108.
4. Richard J. Whalen, *The Founding Father: The Story of Joseph P. Kennedy* (New York, 1964), p. 429. See also Reeves, *A Question of Character,* p. 111; and C. David Heymann, *A Woman Named Jackie: An Intimate Biography of Jacqueline Bouvier Kennedy Onassis* (New York, 1989), p. 99.
5. Reeves, *A Question of Character,* p. 112. See also Heymann, *A Woman Named Jackie,* p. 108.
6. Heymann, *A Woman Named Jackie,* pp. 109–110.

7. Ibid, pp. 130–131.
8. David Burner, *John F. Kennedy and a New Generation* (Boston, 1988), p. 29. See also Reeves, *A Question of Character,* p. 115.
9. Thomas P. O'Neill with William Novak, *Man of the House* (New York, 1987), p. 90.
10. Burner, *John F. Kennedy and a New Generation,* p. 29.
11. Whalen, *The Founding Father,* pp. 429–430.
12. Reeves, *A Question of Character,* p. 123.
13. Sorensen, *Kennedy,* p. 49.
14. Peter Collier and David Horowitz, *The Kennedys: An American Drama* (New York, 1984), p. 205.
15. Burner, *John. F. Kennedy and a New Generation,* p. 30.
16. Whalen, *The Founding Father,* p. 431. See also Reeves, *A Question of Character,* p. 127; and James MacGregor Burns, *John Kennedy: A Political Profile* (New York, 1959), p. 160.
17. John F. Kennedy, *Profiles in Courage* (New York, 1963), p. xx.
18. Sorensen, *Kennedy,* pp. 68–69.
19. Burns, *John Kennedy,* p. 163. See also Reeves, *A Question of Character,* p. 127.
20. Heymann, *A Woman Named Jackie,* p. 184.
21. Burner, *John F. Kennedy and a New Generation,* p. 33.
22. Reeves, *A Question of Character,* p. 135.
23. Kenneth P. O'Donnell and David F. Powers with Joe McCarthy, *"Johnny, We Hardly Knew Ye": Memories of John Fitzgerald Kennedy* (New York, 1973), p. 142.
24. Heymann, *A Woman Named Jackie,* p. 184.
25. O'Donnell and Powers with McCarthy, *"Johnny, We Hardly Knew Ye,"* p. 146.
26. Doris Kearns Goodwin, *The Fitzgeralds and the Kennedys: An American Saga* (New York, 1987), p. 789.
27. Burns, *John Kennedy,* p. 210.
28. Ibid., p. 212.
29. Kearns Goodwin, *The Fitzgeralds and the Kennedys,* p. 794.

5

KENNEDY VERSUS NIXON
The Election of 1960

> " . . . We stand today on the edge of a New Frontier . . ."

It seemed apparent that Richard M. Nixon, Eisenhower's vice president, would easily get the Republican nomination for president. The liberal wing of the Republican Party, headed by Governor Nelson Rockefeller of New York, was not well-organized enough beyond New York State to do very much to stop Nixon. Rockefeller did not hide the fact that he was interested in the presidency, and although he seemed rather like a reluctant bride, hoping that some way would be found to make a marriage between him and his largely conservative party, he did not actively discourage the formation of Citizens for Rockefeller clubs around the country. It was also no secret that Rockefeller disliked Nixon intensely, and that he considered him to be incapable of fulfilling the important role of president. "I hate the thought of Dick Nixon being President of the United States," Rockefeller once told a close friend.[1]

Nevertheless, Nixon had a firm grip on the large middle base of the Republican Party. His eight years as vice president under the popular Eisenhower had served him well. In that time Nixon had traveled the length and breadth of the country speaking to any big-city or small-town Republican group that invited him. He had done political favors for many Republicans and had kept careful lists of all the men and women he had met over the years. Thus, Nixon had amassed numerous friends and supporters. He had stacked up political debts that were owed to him from every corner of the nation. And Richard

Nixon was the kind of politician who always made certain to collect on his political debts.

In order to be nominated in 1960, a Democratic candidate had to show that he could exploit the voters highly negative perceptions of Nixon. Nixon was well known, and had impressed many Americans favorably with his famous "kitchen debate" with the Soviet leader Nikita Khrushchev during a 1959 visit he made to the American exhibit in Moscow.[2]

Still, many Americans distrusted Nixon, who had earned the nickname "Tricky Dick" because of campaign dirty tricks in his early political career in California. This made it difficult for Adlai Stevenson, the Democratic candidate in 1952 and 1956, who had already faced the Republicans in two losing presidential contests with Nixon on the ticket. Stevenson remained the darling of liberal Democrats and intellectuals, but his remarkable wit and intellect carried little weight with the big-city bosses. The party bosses saw Stevenson as a loser, and smelled a Democratic victory in the air if, somehow, the party went with the right candidate in 1960.

There were a number of likely candidates for the Democratic nomination for president that year. Stuart Symington of Missouri was a likable and competent senator. He came from the right geographic location (an industrialized, heartland border state). With his silver hair and handsome face, Symington had the presidential appearance that many American voters equated with competence. However, the only real asset Symington had in a political sense was the fact that former president Harry Truman, a Missouri native from Independence, was his political patron.[3]

The Senate majority leader, Lyndon Baines Johnson of Texas, had a much better chance to win the nomination. He was supported by the powerful speaker of the House, Representative Sam Rayburn. But Johnson had a number of drawbacks. He was unpopular in his home state of Texas, and he was a considered a southerner. It must be remembered that in 1960 southerners, Catholics, blacks and Jews were thought to be incapable of winning national elections. Also, for the first time in American political history, a generation gap appeared. Lyndon Johnson represented the old Democratic Party—that loose and somewhat ineffective coalition of aging reformers from the party of Franklin D. Roosevelt and the New Deal.

These old men were seen by the ambitious, younger Democrats as remnants of the Democratic Party of the past, when deals were made to distribute political power and patronage (jobs) in smoke-filled back rooms of big-city hotels.[4]

Senator Hubert Horatio Humphrey of Minnesota was by far the most impressive candidate of those Democrats who thirsted for victory in the presidential sweepstakes of 1960. Humphrey had many friends, was enormously well-liked and had the backing of a number of important labor unions. In 1948, long before anyone had heard of him on a national level, Humphrey had performed impressively as mayor of Minneapolis when he led the floor fight for civil rights at the Democratic National Convention. Humphrey had hoped to be Stevenson's choice for vice president in 1956. When his political idol Stevenson opened the nomination for the convention to make the choice, a friend found the disconsolate Humphrey weeping. Humphrey's major problem, aside from the fact that he had little money and was known as the party's leading liberal, was that he often wore his emotions on his sleeve. Still, by 1960 Humphrey, who had been largely ignored by the national press in the years of his political growth, was now considered a candidate of substance and a person to respect.

Humphrey's picture had been on the cover of *Time* after the Democratic congressional sweep of 1958. He began to sense that he had some clout in the party, and in 1959 Adlai Stevenson told him that "he was the kind of man the country needed." He sounded out Lyndon Johnson, and Johnson told Humphrey to go ahead—that he himself had no ambitions for the White House. Of course, that was untrue. In addition, Humphrey began to receive many invitations to speak from all over the country—a definite sign that he was a candidate to be taken seriously.[5]

However, the clear front-runner was John F. Kennedy. Kennedy had been reelected to the Senate in 1958 by the largest margin in Massachusetts history and the largest margin of any Democratic senator in that year. He had unlimited funds, important friends from elite universities like Harvard, a large and loyal political organization and, best of all, as the electronic age of mass communication was about to dawn in the United States, Kennedy projected a very positive image before the telling eye of the TV cameras. All that Kennedy seemed to lack were strong political beliefs—at least according to his political enemies.

Hubert Humphrey began to shape up as Kennedy's major obstacle. At a strategy meeting in Duluth, Humphrey's supporters urged the senator to "fish or cut bait." He decided to fish. Humphrey instructed his team to begin to form a presidential committee. His immediate problem was money—he could expect few big donations, and that meant that small donations to the Humphrey campaign would have to be raised in large numbers. This was a difficult political task, since in those days it took as much time and trouble to acquire a small political donation as it did to get a large one. Still, Humphrey was not discouraged. The ever-ebullient Minnesota senator later recalled, "I felt as competent as any man to be President with the exception of Stevenson, but even then I was being compared to Kennedy constantly, and his publicity was incredible it was so good."[6]

The first real match between the Kennedy and Humphrey forces came in the Wisconsin primary. Primaries are the ritual presidential popularity polls that are held in most states every four years to test the political waters and to choose delegates pledged to candidates at the national convention. It appeared, on the surface, that Humphrey had an edge in Wisconsin. Since both senators from Wisconsin were Republicans, Humphrey was often called the third senator from Wisconsin—a neighbor-state to Minnesota, where he had helped many of the dairy farmers and small-town residents. Humphrey also depended heavily on the state's largest concentration of Democrats, in Milwaukee, where he had very good ties with the labor unions.

But all of Humphrey's assets in Wisconsin were not enough. The Kennedy family and political machine descended on Wisconsin like an advancing army. Senator Humphrey was forced to tour the state in a bus while John F. Kennedy's campaign rented a private plane that moved him rapidly and comfortably from one Wisconsin town to another. While Humphrey had offices in only two of the state's ten congressional districts, Kennedy had offices in eight.

In addition, their personalities were very different. Humphrey always talked too much and too long about specific issues. As a result, voters often found themselves either confused or bored. Kennedy, on the other hand, concentrated on his image as the battle in Wisconsin turned increasingly toward the candidate who could purchase the most television time. That candidate was Kennedy. The dean of that era's presidential campaign journalists, Theodore H. White, recalled, "Over and over again there was the handsome, open-faced candidate on the TV screen, showing himself, proving that a Catholic wears no horns."[7]

Kennedy won in Wisconsin with 56% of the vote, carrying six of the state's ten districts. But Kennedy was hardly overjoyed with his victory when it was determined that the Catholic vote had provided the crucial margin. In Protestant areas of the state Kennedy had done poorly. The question looming over the Kennedy campaign after the Wisconsin primary was the old issue of whether a Roman Catholic could be elected to the presidency.

Humphrey misread the results in Wisconsin. Since he had done moderately well with the Catholic vote in Wisconsin, he felt sure that he could take Kennedy on and beat him in West Virginia, the political battleground for the next state primary. The state of West Virginia had a population that was 95% Protestant. It wasn't that Humphrey was a bigot—in fact, he did his best to avoid the religious issue. But he could hardly avoid concluding that Kennedy would not do well with non-Catholics.

Also, Humphrey came out of the Wisconsin campaign heavily in debt; it effectively marked the end of his bid for the presidency. The Kennedys threw all their vast resources into the West Virginia primary. Former president Harry Truman would later say, "Joe [Kennedy] thought of everything. Joe paid for everything."

The Kennedys had never before seen the kind of grinding poverty they saw in West Virginia, and the candidate and his staff couldn't help but be touched by the impoverished people they met as they campaigned across the state. Still, the goal of a political contest is to win. Kennedy money poured into the state and, at times, the campaign got down and dirty. Franklin D. Roosevelt, Jr., the son of the late president, campaigned for Kennedy and raised the ugly issue that Humphrey had not served in World War II. Even though Humphrey had been turned down for medical reasons, the issue surely hurt him.

One angry Charleston newspaper called it "one of the worst name-calling campaigns in the history of presidential politics."

Another local newspaper charged that the Kennedys had engaged in vote-buying on a massive scale and stated that the primary was "One of the most corrupt elections in county history." For years the Kennedys had funneled money into the pockets of West Virginia Democratic state and local office holders. Local sheriffs got an average of $1,000 in cash to help the Kennedy effort.

The Kennedy army of volunteers spread across the state for door-to-door distribution of campaign materials; rural mailings; a well-organized telephone campaign; ox roasts and weenie roasts similar to the polite teas in Massachusetts; and personal visits by the handsome candidate and his family. Humphrey didn't have a chance.

On May 10, Kennedy buried Humphrey with 61% of the vote, putting to rest the idea that a Catholic could not appeal to Protestant voters. A man in front of the Putnam County Courthouse seemed to sum up the thinking of the typical West Virginia voter when he said, "I'm a Baptist, but I got nothing against no man's religion."

With his eyes glistening with tears under the bright TV lights, Hubert Humphrey entered his main headquarters in Charleston accompanied by Bobby Kennedy, who represented his brother. "I have a brief statement," Humphrey said. "I am no longer a candidate for the Democratic presidential nomination."

Sixteen years later, when Humphrey published his memoirs, he had still not gotten over the bitter taste left from the primaries of 1960 and his battle with the Kennedys. Humphrey wrote,

> As a professional politician, I was able to accept and indeed respect the efficacy of the Kennedy campaign. But underneath the beautiful exterior, there was an element of ruthlessness and toughness that I had trouble either accepting or forgetting.[8]

In the first week of July the action shifted to Los Angeles for the inside political fight that is the Democratic Party's national nominating convention. Under unusually smogless blue skies some 4,509 delegates were outnumbered by 4,750 representatives of the news media, along with hundreds of party officials and workers.

On the eighth floor of the Biltmore Hotel, the Kennedy command operation was set up in four rooms—Suite 8315. The Kennedy team represented a new generation of bold young men who stood on the verge of changing the path of history. The chief of staff was Robert F. Kennedy, the candidate's brother, age 34; Kenneth P. O'Donnell, a World War II bomber-navigator, was 36; Pierre Salinger, the campaign's liaison to the press, was 36; and the grand old man of the Kennedy inner circle, Lawrence F. O'Brien of Springfield, Massachusetts, was 43.

The Kennedy forces counted 600 certain votes on the first ballot. However, they knew they needed at least 700 votes to ensure a first-ballot victory. If Kennedy were held under 700 votes, there was a chance that on a second ballot his support would begin to fade. With their work cut out for them, the Kennedy troops swung into action on the convention floor.

Using vastly improved technology that had not been at their disposal at the 1956 convention, the Kennedy forces strung their own independent network of communications between the floor of the convention and their headquarters at the Biltmore. Robert Kennedy would give an instant command and a Kennedy worker would be quickly dispatched to the floor to bargain, plead or make a deal with the various power brokers in the state delegations.

The powerful boss of Cook County in Illinois, Chicago Mayor Richard Daley, was the first to break ranks. Daley had been an old friend and political ally of Governor Stevenson. But Joseph Kennedy had extensive real estate holdings in Chicago and had a great deal of influence on Daley, who always liked to be with winners. During a secret caucus Daley saw to it that the Illinois delegation's votes went 59½ for Kennedy and only two for Stevenson. That effectively broke the logjam for Kennedy votes, as other delegations like Pennsylvania and Ohio were brought into line by the state party bosses and the Kennedy operatives on the convention floor.

Even though Stevenson was nominated—in an eloquent speech by Senator Eugene McCarthy, who said, "Do not reject this man who has made us all proud to be Democrats. Do not leave this prophet without honor in his own party"—the

Kennedy organization was too powerful and well-organized to be overcome. Kennedy received the nomination on the first ballot with 806 votes. Lyndon Johnson, who had been trapped in Washington carrying out his senatorial duties and did not campaign, came in second with 409 votes.

On Friday, Kennedy appeared before the convention to deliver his acceptance speech. More important, some 35 million Americans watched the proceedings on TV. The electronic age in American politics had begun.

He spoke in general terms about the nation's problems, noting that "we stand today on the edge of a New Frontier—a frontier of unknown opportunities and perils—a frontier of unfulfilled hopes and threats."[9]

Everyone was surprised when Kennedy chose Lyndon Johnson as his vice-presidential running mate. The two men had become bitter rivals in the spring primaries and did not like one another very much. Robert Kennedy especially disliked Johnson, and some labor leaders worried that picking a southerner would alienate the black vote.

However, the Kennedy strategy was a good one. With Johnson on the ticket the Democrats now had two of the three major elements of the party on board: the South, since Johnson was a southerner; and the big-city political leaders. The third element, labor, had nowhere else to go and would never vote Republican anyway.

The Republicans met the next month at their convention in Chicago and, as expected, nominated Vice President Richard M. Nixon. While Kennedy had burst on the American scene as a relative newcomer, most Americans had an opinion about Richard Nixon. Over the years he had made many enemies, and a lot of voters disliked him intensely. Yet, if Nixon was not universally loved, he was admired by middle-class America. His political rise from an impoverished working-class Quaker background was the classic American success story. Nixon and Kennedy had entered Congress together and knew one another. Kennedy said, "Nixon is a nice fellow in private and a very able man. I worked with him on the Hill for a long time, but he seems to have a split personality; and he is very bad in public, and nobody likes him."[10]

Nixon would run on the Eisenhower record of peace and prosperity. He represented small-town America and was a man who had retained many small-town virtues and prejudices. Even though Nixon was to be the candidate of big business, he had become a politician with few firmly held beliefs. He would take almost any position on an issue if he felt he could gain from it politically. Most important, Nixon was not a Catholic.

However, Nixon made some fatal mistakes that would hurt him in the campaign. He did not trust many people, and had been used to controlling his own affairs as a congressman, senator and even as vice president. A national political campaign in the modern political era could hardly be managed with any ultimate success by the candidate himself, who had to busy himself with the mentally and physically grueling demands of mastering the issues, delivering speeches, and making countless numbers of public appearances all over the country during the tight and hectic schedule of a short presidential campaign.

In 1860, after receiving the Republican nomination for president, Abraham Lincoln went home to Illinois. It was then considered unseemly for a candidate to campaign for high public office. Exactly a century later, with the birth of the modern presidential campaign, everything had changed. By promising to campaign in all 50 states Nixon literally wore himself out.

But Nixon's biggest mistake was to agree to an unprecedented series of nationally televised debates with Kennedy. These debates would alter the American political landscape and change political campaigning for the rest of the century.

Clearly, Nixon didn't understand where electronic journalism was heading in 1960. He told writer Earl Mazo in 1959, "Television is not so effective now as it was in 1952. The novelty has worn off."[11]

Nixon had been a champion debater in college, and he totally underestimated Kennedy's skills. Kennedy saw the debates as a chance to show himself off to the press and to the American people. He was surprised that Nixon had accepted his challenge, and said that Nixon was "a damn fool to agree to debate me on an equal-time TV basis. Just imagine if Eisenhower had had to do this against Stevenson in 1952 and 1956. He would have looked silly."[12]

Kennedy prepared for the debates as if he were studying for final examinations in college. Two days before each debate, Kennedy's legislative assistant Mike Feldman would bring him a stack of briefing papers. On the day of the debate, Feldman, Theodore Sorensen, and Richard Goodwin, a brilliant 28-year-old graduate of Harvard Law School, would spend hours rehearsing key points and concepts with Kennedy. Each night before he went to bed Kennedy would scan cards filled with facts and statistics that his team had carefully prepared. Kennedy would study thousands of pages dealing with Nixon's policies and views.[13]

Why were the TV debates so important in 1960? In 1950 only 11% of American families owned a TV set. By 1960 88% of Americans had a TV set. Thus, if you went on TV in 1950 you could hope to reach perhaps 4,400,000 people. In 1960 that number had skyrocketed: by going on national television a politician could reach as many as 40 million Americans in a single program. What Richard Nixon did not understand was the fact that the American people watched television on an average of four to five hours each day and that the hours of viewing time were growing.[14]

The four debates were scattered throughout the fall: on September 26 in Chicago; October 7 in Washington; October 13 in New York; and October 21, again in New York. All three networks—ABC, CBS and NBC—participated. And when the debates were over the network executives were amazed. Each broadcast had averaged an audience of between 65 and 70 million American viewers.

The first debate in Chicago was the most important, because it set the tone for the ones that followed. The visual contrast on TV between the two men was powerful. Kennedy appeared calm and confident. He projected an image of youth and glamorous vigor. Nixon, still recovering from an August knee operation, was tired, tense and, at times, even looked frightened on television. Nixon had refused any makeup, and because he had a dark complexion to begin with, looked on the flickering black-and-white screen as if he had forgotten to shave (it must be remembered that this was before color TV). Nixon ignored the audience, directing his attention to Kennedy as if he were being scored by a college debate panel; Kennedy, in full control, addressed the audience that really counted: the nation. Kennedy opened on a statesmanlike note similar to the one that Abraham Lincoln had sounded during the Civil War era. Referring to the enormous influence the Soviets exercised in

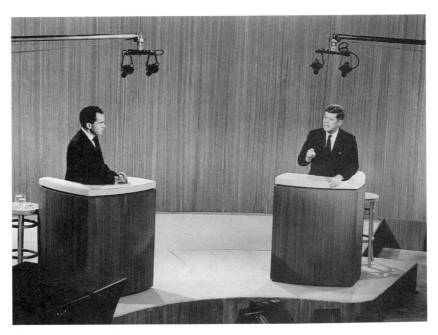

The Kennedy-Nixon debate, 1960 (John F. Kennedy Library)

international affairs, Kennedy maintained that the world could not endure half-slave and half-free.

Nixon opened by agreeing with Kennedy's statement, but he spent far too much time praising the progress made under the Eisenhower presidency and not enough outlining his own ideas of government.

Perhaps it did not really matter what Nixon said. It was what Americans saw that ultimately counted. Theodore H. White, covering the debates, reveals what Americans saw on TV that night:

> the Vice President as he half slouched, his "Lazy Shave" powder faintly streaked with sweat, his eyes exaggerated hollows of blackness, his jaw, jowls, and face drooping with strain. . . . His normal shirt hung loosely about his neck, and his recent weight loss made him appear scrawny.

In the end the Kennedy-Nixon debates had little to do with issues, even though both candidates were well prepared for battle. The debates focused more on the personalities and images that were projected on the TV screen. Kennedy wore a well-tailored dark suit, while Nixon wore a light suit that seemed to melt his weakened image into the black-and-white TV screens of America.

Noting the emphasis on imagery, Theodore H. White complained, "rarely in American history has there been a political campaign that discussed issues less or clarified them less. The TV debates . . . were the greatest opportunity ever for such a discussion, but it was an opportunity missed."[15]

Most polls taken after the first debate gave the victory to Kennedy. However, it was interesting that most of those who listened to the debate on the radio believed that Nixon had won. The most extensive poll, conducted for CBS by Dr. Elmo Roper, found that of four million Americans who had been decisively influenced by the TV debates, three million voted for Kennedy while one million voted for Nixon. And as Kennedy himself said after the election, "It was TV more than anything else that turned the tide."[16]

Although Nixon recovered somewhat in the later debates, no audience was as large as the first. Years later Nixon admitted making crucial errors in the debates. He said, "I had lost two weeks of campaigning to a knee injury that kept me in the hospital, and so I felt I had to make up for lost time. On the day of the crucial first debate with Jack Kennedy, I agreed to an appearance before a carpenters' union convention. . . . I did not feel tired but I looked tired, and I had foolishly not put on makeup to compensate for the bags under my eyes and my five-o'clock shadow. Kennedy might have won the election anyway. But my failure to use time properly could have made a difference."[17]

The TV debates, perhaps more than anything else, set a precedent in American political history. Arriving at the precise moment when the first TV generation was coming of voting age, they would ensure that televised debates would play a role in presidential politics for the rest of the century.

For his part, Kennedy was bolstered by the debates and he campaigned with renewed vigor greeted by growing crowds across the country. Kennedy told Professor John Kenneth Galbraith of Harvard, "When I first began this campaign, I just wanted to beat Nixon. Now I want to save the country from him."[18]

In November, although the popular vote was very close, with only 112,000 votes separating Kennedy and Nixon, Kennedy defeated Nixon 303 to 219 in the electoral college. Kennedy was undoubtedly helped by the switching of crucial votes by some of the Democratic bosses in Texas and Illinois—especially in Mayor Richard Daley's Cook County, where the early-morning returns coming out of key Chicago precincts just tilted the state in favor of Kennedy. To his credit, Richard Nixon did not contest the election—an action that would have thrown the country into turmoil.[19]

John F. Kennedy had been elected president by a very narrow margin, less than 1% of the popular vote. He had put together a winning Democratic coalition that brought the Republican ascendancy under Dwight D. Eisenhower to a close.

That coalition included black Americans. The Kennedy brothers had boldly intervened when civil rights leader Dr. Martin Luther King, Jr. was arrested for a traffic offense and sentenced to six months in a Georgia prison. Kennedy called King's wife, Coretta, to express his concern for King's safety. Then his brother Robert called a Georgia judge to help arrange for Dr. King to be released on bond. Black Americans never forgot what the Kennedys had done, and repaid them handsomely at the voting booths. Seven out of ten blacks voted for Kennedy, and in black urban areas the tally was even higher. In Detroit, for example, Kennedy beat Nixon eight to one in the black community.[20]

American Catholics too voted preponderantly for Kennedy. In the states in the Northeast that had big cities with large Catholic populations, the Catholic vote was vital to Kennedy's victory. Kennedy may have defused the anti-Catholic feeling in the country when he wisely appeared before the Greater Houston Ministerial Association in Texas during the campaign. Raising the religion issue himself, Kennedy told the meeting of Protestant ministers, "I believe in an America where the separation of church and state is absolute—where no Catholic prelate would tell the President (should he be a Catholic) how to act and no Protestant minister would tell his parishioners for whom to vote."[21]

The president and his brothers: left to right, JFK, Robert F. Kennedy, Edward M. Kennedy (John F. Kennedy Library)

Thus, for the first time in American history, a Catholic candidate scored heavily with Protestant voters. Kennedy actually ended up with more Protestant votes than Nixon. And eight out of ten American Jews voted for Kennedy. According to one scholar, "The near solidarity of anti-Nixon sentiment among Jews in states like New York and Illinois may have resulted in the Kennedy victory."[22] Clearly, the American Jewish community did not hold Joseph P. Kennedy's overt anti-Semitism against his son.

The only region of the country where Nixon did well was the South, where he was still able to play up to the small-town and rural mentality that fueled a strong resentment of the big-city Democratic machine politicians. And, of course, there was the ingrained fear in the South that the election of John F. Kennedy would signal a change in race relations in that region. The civil rights movement, still in its infancy, was stirring, and many southerners feared that with John F. Kennedy in the White House, relations between the races would somehow be drastically altered.

In the end the election of 1960 was a triumph of personality— John F. Kennedy's over Richard M. Nixon's. The Democratic Party's philosophy that government is to be used as a tool to help the citizens collided head-on with the Republican Party philosophy that argued that every citizen must bear some responsibility for his or her own well-being. But these heady philosophical issues were lost in the glitz and glitter of a media-inspired campaign that, on the surface at least, revolved around the image and personalities of the two candidates.

Neither Kennedy nor Nixon was an ideologue or a true believer in his party's political dogma. More than anything else they were both highly ambitious politicians who tried to work the system. One failed and one succeeded in 1960. But the American political system had worked. In their wisdom the American people had narrowly chosen John F. Kennedy to lead them into a new decade. What nobody could have known was that the advent of Kennedy to the presidency would also signal a new and dangerously tumultuous era in American history.

Notes

1. Theodore H. White, *The Making of the President 1960* (New York, 1961), pp. 68–71.
2. Michael Kort, *Nikita Khrushchev* (New York, 1989), p. 119.
3. White, *The Making of the President 1960,* pp. 38–39.
4. Ibid., pp. 43–46.
5. Ibid., pp. 29–30.
6. Ibid., p. 32.

7. Quoted in Thomas C. Reeves, *A Question of Character: A Life of John F. Kennedy* (New York, 1991), p. 164; and William L. O'Neill, *Coming Apart: An Informal History of America in the 1960's* (Chicago, 1971), p. 15.

8. David Burner, *John F. Kennedy and a New Generation* (Boston, 1988), pp. 48–49. See also White, *The Making of the President 1960,* pp. 99–114; and quoted in Victor Lasky, *It Didn't Start With Watergate* (New York, 1977), pp. 31–33.

9. White, *The Making of the President 1960,* p. 155, p. 160, p. 165, p. 169, and p. 177.

10. Ralph G. Martin, *A Hero for Our Time: An Intimate Story of the Kennedy Years* (New York, 1983), p. 195.

11. Earl Mazo, *Richard Nixon: A Political and Personal Portrait* (New York, 1959), p. 299. See also O'Neill, *Coming Apart,* p. 21.

12. Martin, *A Hero for Our Time,* p. 195.

13. White, *The Making of the President 1960,* pp. 283–285.

14. Ibid., pp. 279–280.

15. Ibid., pp. 287–292.

16. Ibid., p. 294.

17. Richard Nixon, *In the Arena: A Memoir of Victory, Defeat and Renewal* (New York, 1990), p. 122.

18. Martin, *A Hero for Our Time,* p. 197.

19. Burner, *John F. Kennedy and a New Generation,* p. 55.

20. White, *The Making of the President 1960,* p. 323 and p. 354.

21. Lawrence H. Fuchs, *John F. Kennedy and American Catholicism* (New York, 1967), p. 179.

22. White, *The Making of the President 1960,* pp. 350–360; and quoted in Stephen D. Isaacs, *Jews and American Politics* (New York, 1974), p. 158.

6

A POOR START
JFK and the Bay of Pigs

"The worse I do, the more popular I get."

On January 17, 1961, President Dwight D. Eisenhower left the presidency with a stern warning for his fellow citizens about the growing power of the military-industrial complex in America. But Eisenhower's well-chosen words were lost in the glare of the spotlight on the new First Family and the excitement that it brought to the formation of a new government.

From his stirring inaugural address to the gala inaugural balls and parties choreographed by Hollywood celebrities like Frank Sinatra, the initial weeks of John F. Kennedy's presidency had a dreamlike quality to them. As Theodore H. White recalled, "It was all gay in the first few weeks, all aglitter, all bravado. Yet it comes to me now that underneath the bravado, he, like all new Presidents, was groping."[1]

President-elect Kennedy had spent the time between his election and his inauguration carefully selecting a team of men to help him run the nation. He gave plum ambassadorial posts to his old mentors and teachers from Harvard University: Professor John Kenneth Galbraith was appointed ambassador to India, and Professor Edwin Reischauer was made ambassador to Japan. Adlai Stevenson, who had faithfully carried the banner of the Democratic Party twice in the 1950s without success, was made ambassador to the United Nations.

However, the true men of power in the Kennedy administration were the men (and they were all men) selected by Kennedy to serve in his cabinet. Orville Freeman, former governor of

Minnesota, was named secretary of agriculture. Luther Hodges, who had served as governor of North Carolina, was secretary of commerce. R. Sargent Shriver, who had no special qualifications beyond the fact that he was a Kennedy brother-in-law married to sister Eunice and had helped to assemble the new administration, was awarded the non-cabinet job of head of the Peace Corps, an innovative program that was instituted to allow Americans to perform community service in Third World nations. Douglas Dillon, a holdover from the Eisenhower administration, was treasury secretary. Arthur Goldberg, a brilliant labor lawyer, was made secretary of labor. Abraham Ribicoff, an early Kennedy supporter and governor of Connecticut, was made secretary of health, education and welfare.

Robert McNamara was a key man in the Kennedy cabinet. The former head of the Ford Motor Company became secretary of defense. Dean Rusk, head of the powerful Rockefeller Foundation, whose appointment was supported by former secretary of state Dean Acheson, became the new secretary of state. Kennedy wondered whether Rusk was sufficiently "tough-fibered." It wouldn't take long before the president was to find out.

Kennedy's most important appointment also turned out to be his most controversial. Kennedy shocked all of official Washington when he announced that brother Robert would serve as attorney general, the nation's chief law enforcement officer.

Other key appointments to the Kennedy inner circle included Theodore Sorensen, Kenneth P. O'Donnell, and Dave Powers, who served on the White House staff; Pierre Salinger, who was made press secretary; and Harvard University professor McGeorge Bundy, who was given the title of special assistant to the president for national security affairs. Other presidential advisers included Walt Rostow and General Maxwell D. Taylor.[2]

Who were these powerful and successful men? As historian William L. O'Neill writes, "They were not so much liberals as technocrats, men of power rather than passion. Unsentimental, except about the President (and sometimes each other), they made a fetish of energy and style."[3]

President Kennedy didn't have much time to enjoy the glitter of his inauguration press. His first struggle, with Congress, indicated that Kennedy would have difficulty getting his legislative program approved. The problem was that of the 261 Democrats in the House, 101 were from southern or border states. These representatives, mostly conservatives, were closer to the Republican Party on most issues than they were to their own party. Thus, in the first few months of his presidency Kennedy's domestic programs could barely get off the ground. However, if Kennedy's achievements on the domestic level were initially dismal, his foreign policy was nothing less than disastrous.

What happened to the Kennedy administration in the area of foreign affairs was not entirely the fault of the new president. Many of the problems had been inherited from the Eisenhower administration—especially those concerning the island of Cuba, only 90 miles off the coast of Florida.

During the 1960 campaign Kennedy had attacked Nixon and the Eisenhower administration for allowing communism to flourish in Cuba. In 1959 and early 1960, following the successful overthrow of United States–backed Cuban dictator Fulgencio Batista by Fidel Castro, tens of thousands of Cuban refugees streamed into Miami. For a time, many Americans saw Castro as an enigmatic revolutionary who had liberated his people—a Cuban Robin Hood who had heroically conducted a guerrilla war from the mountainous countryside against the evil and corrupt Batista. The Batista regime, supported by powerful American corporate interests in combination with some of the most sinister elements of U.S. organized crime, had bled Cuba and its large peasant population dry.[4]

When Castro finally took power, his chief lieutenant, Ernesto "Che" Guevara, speaking to a youth Congress in Havana in August, 1960, clarified the Cuban revolution. Guevara said:

> What is our ideology? If I were asked whether our revolution is Communist, I would define it as Marxist.[5]

It did not take Castro long to announce to the world that he was a Communist. The Eisenhower administration immediately swung into action. In 1959 an economic embargo was declared against Cuba. The Central Intelligence Agency (CIA), the highly covert government agency begun after World War II mainly to counter Soviet operations in all parts of the world, was secretly authorized to begin training 1,200 Cuban exiles on the Pacific coast of Guatemala. Ultimately, Eisenhower's goal was to put some 700 Cubans ashore in Cuba to begin guerrilla warfare against Castro and his Communist regime. Of course, during the campaign, Kennedy was unaware of all of this. When Kennedy asked Eisenhower, in a briefing during the campaign, whether any American operations were underway, Eisenhower alluded to the Cubans being trained in Guatemala. But he led Kennedy to believe that the CIA operation had nothing to do with U.S. troops or with foreign policy.[6]

By 1961, when Kennedy took office, over 100,000 Cuban emigrés had entered the United States. Meanwhile, back in Cuba, Castro had closed off many avenues of emigration and had executed over 500 of his opponents by firing squad. When questioned about his brutality and about Cuba's failure to hold free elections, Castro reportedly told Richard Nixon, "The people of Cuba don't want free elections; they produce bad government. The people of Cuba don't want them to have fair trials. They want them shot as quickly as possible."[7]

While Kennedy continued the Eisenhower policy of secretly training Cuban troops in Guatemala, he gave the impression publicly that there was little the United States could do about Castro. In early February Kennedy sent Arthur M. Schlesinger, Jr. to meet with the presidents of six Latin American countries. Schlesinger, a Pulitzer Prize-winning Harvard University historian, had been brought onto the White House staff as a "special assistant." The president asked Schlesinger to find out whether the Latin American leaders would be upset if the Cuban exiles attempted to get rid of Castro. Schlesinger was supposed to be briefed by Richard Bissell, the CIA agent in charge of the Cuban operations. However, Bissell never actually told Schlesinger of the CIA's intentions.

Convinced that an American attempt to overthrow Fidel Castro "would fix a malevolent image of the new Administration in the minds of millions," Schlesinger wrote a series of memorandums to President Kennedy warning against taking any drastic action against Cuba.[8]

But Kennedy had apparently made up his mind long before the inauguration, and Schlesinger's memorandums had little impact on his thinking. On November 29, 1960, Kennedy had been briefed by CIA director Allen Dulles about the Cuban operations. The president-elect listened carefully and instructed Dulles to go ahead with the Cuban project. By December a plan was presented at the CIA before the Special Group— a secret CIA interdepartmental committee that was put in charge of the Cuban operations. Thus, even before Kennedy was in office and before the new administration had had an opportunity to formulate its own policy, the CIA was developing a plan of operations to deal with Castro.

The CIA plan was for 650 to 750 Cubans to go ashore somewhere along the southeast shoreline of the island. To soften up the emigré landing, air strikes were supposed to be launched from Guatemala to knock out Cuba's tiny air force. The objective of the invaders would be to seize and hold a large enough area on the island so that the anti-Castro activists who were still in Cuba would rise up, foment defections from Castro's special militia units, and then spark a general uprising throughout the island.

The CIA was assured by the Cubans that the troops training in Guatemala were of high caliber, highly intelligent, highly motivated, and that their morale was high. It would have been far more accurate simply to describe them as high—because many of the Cuban troops, bored with hours of dull training and the loneliness of isolated jungle life, took to drugs and liquor.

The CIA's Special Group had made a serious mistake. Because members of the Special Group didn't want to give up their bureaucratic role in the struggle to control important events, they did not formally approve the Cuban invasion scheme. At the same time, they did not subject the invasion plan to severe analysis. Had they done so they would have found out that the 1,400 Cubans training in Guatemala were not prepared or equipped to deal with Castro's large standing army, which numbered a quarter of a million troops and was well equipped by the Soviet Union to meet the threat of outside invasion.

Instead, the CIA was encouraged to proceed on two fronts: train Cuban troops in Guatemala, and prepare a plan of military operations. Clearly, the CIA was playing it safe. If the operation went ahead, the agency wanted it to appear to be a Cuban activity—one that was planned, manned, financed and ultimately carried out by the Cuban exiles. Thus, if it failed, only Cubans would be held strictly accountable. What the CIA did not figure into the equation was the important fact that final responsibility for success or failure would fall on the shoulders of President Kennedy.

For his part, President Kennedy saw the initial CIA plan as far "too spectacular." Kennedy said, "This is too much like a World War II invasion." What Kennedy wanted was a quiet night landing on Cuba, if possible, without any American military participation.[9]

Meanwhile, the CIA Operational Support Division had begun to explore the possibility of assassinating Fidel Castro. In one of the strangest alliances in modern American history, the CIA hired the American mobsters Sam Giancana and Johnny Rosselli to murder the head of a sovereign foreign nation. The gangsters began to develop a number of farfetched schemes, from gunning Castro down to poisoning his food and drink to get rid of him. The gangsters, in a caricature of the then-popular fictional spy James Bond, even developed a number of plots that included poisoned cigars and exploding pens and baseballs that would surely have tested the initiative of the great James Bond himself.[10]

Beyond the fact that the CIA-Mafia plots were ridiculous was the question of their legality. Several questions should have been asked by the CIA. How could a legitimate arm of the United States government involve itself in the murder of a head of state without the direct approval of the president? Turning to the invasion plan itself, did the Cuban amphibious assault forces have a ghost of a chance of conquering Castro's Cuba fighting from the remote and isolated beaches of the Bay of Pigs—a landing site that was far from desirable in a geographic sense? And more important, in terms of American self-interest, could the United States escape accountability for what was about to transpire? If it could not, how could the United States allow such an expedition to fail? Unfortunately, neither the CIA nor, apparently, the president or his military and civilian advisers ever raised these vital questions.

The problem was that President Kennedy relied on the advice of experts. Kennedy's military advisers, General Lyman Lemnitzer of the Army, Admiral Arleigh Burke of the Navy and General Thomas White of the Air Force—the Joint Chiefs of Staff—did nothing to dissuade their commander-in-chief from the folly of the Cuban adventure. In fact, it was they and their key military advisers in the Pentagon who actually selected the Bay of Pigs for the site of the invasion.

The invasion plan was bold and actually fit in very well with the adventurous spirit that both Kennedy brothers fostered in their "New Frontier" philosophy. As one White House aide said,

> Nobody in the White House wanted to be soft. That was the trouble. There were questions about the plan, but it was a fascinating plan. Everybody wanted to show they were just as daring and just as bold as anyone else. They didn't look at it close enough.[11]

Ultimately, the pace of events quickened to the point that they were even beyond the control of the president of the United States. In early March 1961, the president of Guatemala, Miguel Ydigoras, wrote Kennedy that the presence of the Cubans in his country was beginning to become an embarrassment. Ydigoras requested that Kennedy see to it that the Cubans were gone by the end of April. Simultaneously, the CIA reported that the Cuban soldiers were combat-ready, that the spirit of the Brigade was high and that further delay would risk demoralization of the troops. Also, the rainy season was about to begin in Guatemala and that would have prevented further military training as the ground turned into mud. In addition, Castro was about to receive a shipment of jet planes from the Soviet Union with Cuban pilots who had been trained in Czechoslovakia to fly them. Once the planes arrived in Cuba, any invasion by sea would have turned into a slaughter. By the middle of March, Arthur Schlesinger, Jr. notes, "the President was confronted, in effect, with a now-or-never choice."[12]

One of the many problems for the Kennedy administration was the fact that the Cuban operation was proceeding in the open. All attempts at secrecy had apparently failed. Tad Szulc, a reporter for the *New York Times,* filed a story from Miami describing the recruitment of the Cuban soldiers and reporting that a landing on Cuba was imminent. In an attempt to save lives and keep the newspaper from interfering with national policy, Szulc's editors, Turner Catledge and James Reston, killed the story. But it didn't really matter.

Other American newspapers and magazines began to report news of an impending invasion. *The New Republic* had earlier printed accurate information on the Guatemalan training camps and was about to report on the CIA's activities among the Cuban refugees in Miami. At the suggestion of President Kennedy, the magazine did not print the story—but that did not stop the extensive rumor mill between Washington and Miami. The prestige and power of the administration might well stop a story from being printed but it could never prevent the ongoing gossip among editors, reporters and their many contacts. Kennedy's press secretary, Pierre Salinger, called the Bay of Pigs "the least covert military operation in history" and complained, "The only information Castro didn't have was the exact time and place of the invasion." Salinger noted that Kennedy was furious with the leaks and told him, "I can't believe what I'm reading! Castro doesn't need agents over here. All he has to do is read our papers."[13]

By the first week of April 1961 it was clear that the president had decided to go ahead with the invasion plan. Kennedy instructed Arthur Schlesinger on April 7 to brief United Nations ambassador Adlai Stevenson in New York, saying, "The integrity and credibility of Adlai Stevenson constitute one of our great national assets. I don't want anything to be done which might jeopardize that."

Kennedy was apparently convinced by the CIA that the Cuban Brigade could hit the beach and "melt" into the nearby mountains. He believed that a full-scale invading force would not be needed—that the Brigade would, at the very least, be able to remain in the Cuban countryside, from where they could conduct guerrilla operations against the Castro regime. "I don't think we fully realized that the Escambray Mountains lay eighty miles from the Bay of Pigs, across a hopeless tangle of swamps and jungles," said Arthur Schlesinger, Jr.[14]

At a news conference on April 12 President Kennedy assured the press that United States forces would not intervene in Cuba. In effect, Kennedy had tipped his own hand. Fidel Castro, an avid Kennedy watcher, was now certain that an attack on Cuba was about to take place. Although he could not be certain where the main landing would occur, he guessed it would be in the south. As it happened, Castro guessed correctly.

Castro gave instructions to place his regular army units of 25,000 well-trained soldiers and 200,000 militiamen in key strategic spots all over the country. A company of militia was dispatched to the Bay of Pigs. The Americans, it turned out, had seriously underestimated Castro's military and strategic skills.[15]

On April 14 the American advisers disclosed their invasion plan to the administration. Three beaches were to be seized along 40 miles of shoreline in the Bay of Pigs area. Paratroops were to be dropped some miles inland in order to control the roads crossing the swamps to the sea. If the invaders could hold the beaches for three days, it was hoped that word would spread throughout the island and that they would be joined by thousands of Cuban patriots. As the chief American adviser told the Brigade,

> you will be so strong, you will be getting so many people to your side, that you won't want to wait for us. You will go straight ahead. You will put your hands out, turn left, and go straight into Havana.

As the Brigade left in seven small ships from Nicaragua, the dictator Luis Somoza waved goodbye from the dock, shouting loudly, "Bring me a couple of hairs from Castro's beard."[16]

But it was not to be. Although the CIA estimated that Castro's air force had been disabled by the first wave of air strikes on April 15, American U-2 spyplanes showed that only five Cuban planes had definitely been destroyed.

At the United Nations, Ambassador Adlai Stevenson's "briefing" left him almost totally in the dark. Stevenson even read the CIA cover story into the record when he was asked to comment on the air strikes. Secretary of State Dean Rusk was under siege by the media at the State Department. He had already permitted his United Nations ambassador to lie publicly. Now the reporters were calling the State Department to ask penetrating questions about B-26 bombers that had been taking off from airfields in Miami and Key West. What was Rusk to do as the media focused in on the fact that American bomber pilots were involved in the air strikes against Cuba?

Secretary of State Rusk called President Kennedy to tell him that the next projected air strike could not be launched from American soil. The perplexed president, maintaining that the only strike he knew about was to come from the sea, said, "I'm not signed on to this," and canceled the follow-up air strikes. After talking to his secretary of state, Kennedy sat quietly, lost in his own thoughts. Realizing that things were in a general state of confusion, he got up and paced the room. His aides, wrote Arthur Schlesinger, Jr., "had rarely seen him so low."[17]

Kennedy's main concern from that point on was that no American troops become involved in the Cuban invasion. But events had far outdistanced the will of the president of the United States. The Cuban Brigade had already reached the area offshore from the Bay of Pigs. What the commander-in-chief had ordered was not carried out, as American Navy frogmen had landed on the remote beaches to mark off critical invasion points early on April 17. Despite Kennedy's order, the first men to hit those beaches were Americans. The Navy frogmen soon encountered a Cuban militia patrol. All hope of tactical surprise was lost as the Americans and Cubans exchanged rifle fire.

On April 17 the Cuban Brigade went ashore. From their exposed landing craft they could see the flashes of rifle fire that marked the battle between the Americans and the Cuban militia. As they made their way through the dark waters, some of the smaller vessels ran into the coral reefs that dotted the water just off the shore. The pre-invasion CIA briefings had made no mention of the dangerous coral reefs that almost completely protected the entrance to the Bay of Pigs.

Many of the brave Cuban invaders soon found themselves swimming for their lives toward the beaches through shark-infested waters. To make matters worse, the Soviet-trained Cuban air force swept out of the early morning skies, firing 50-caliber machine guns at the men on the ships and strafing the troops that had made it to the beaches. Castro's planes sank two boats before they could reach the beach. One of the boats held all of the Brigade's communication and radio equipment and much of their reserve munitions. As a result, the Cubans who made it to shore had no way to communicate with one another and were already desperately short of equipment.

Castro was personally directing the operation. He knew the Bay of Pigs area well, as it was his favorite fishing spot. In Havana Castro's police arrested 200,000 people and herded them into theaters and auditoriums. Anyone remotely suspected of having connections to the underground was arrested.

Thus, Castro swiftly neutralized the possibility of the wholesale insurrection that the CIA had hoped would sweep the island.[18]

At a 7 A.M. meeting on Tuesday, April 17, in the cabinet room at the White House, President Kennedy's worst fears were confirmed. Walt Rostow and McGeorge Bundy, two of Kennedy's national security assistants, sat with CIA director Allen Dulles and a number of military advisers. Dulles reported that the operation was failing and that the Brigade was trapped on the beaches. Castro was moving a large number of well-equipped troops to surround and overpower them. President Kennedy asked a few questions but said little. He still hoped that perhaps the battle would somehow turn around. But as each hour passed the news grew worse. The pressure was on Kennedy to give the order for American troops to go to the aid of the beleaguered Cuban Brigade.

That night President Kennedy and his wife Jackie hosted the annual congressional reception at the White House. To those who saw him, Kennedy appeared smiling and relaxed as he danced with the First Lady to the Marine band's "Mr. Wonderful." It was a charade.

At midnight the President abruptly excused himself, leaving the reception to attend a meeting in the cabinet room with the Joint Chiefs, the secretaries of defense and state, and the vice president. Richard Bissell of the CIA told Kennedy that the situation was desperate. He suggested that the only way to avoid complete and utter tragedy would be for Kennedy to authorize sending in American jets from the aircraft carrier *Essex*. Kennedy admired Bissell's argument but adamantly refused. Admiral Arleigh Burke then argued in favor of bringing in an American destroyer. Later Burke said, "One destroyer opening fire could have knocked the hell out of Castro's tanks. It might have changed the whole course of the battle."

But again, the president refused. "I don't want the United States involved in this," he told Burke angrily.

The meeting lasted until almost 3 A.M. Kennedy was devastated. Kenneth O'Donnell said he "had never seen him so distraught" and that the president had "come as close to crying" as he had ever seen him.[19] A few days later Kennedy wondered aloud to Theodore Sorensen: "How could I have been so far off base? All my life I've known better than to depend on the experts. How could I have been so stupid, to let them go ahead?"[20]

The Bay of Pigs invasion turned into a colossal failure. Of the 1,500 men who made up the Brigade, 114 were killed, 1,189 were captured, and 150 either didn't land or somehow made their way off the deadly beaches and out of the snake-infested swamps.[21]

The Bay of Pigs fiasco resulted from a combination of factors based on false assumptions. A youthful and inexperienced American president, schooled in the public relations tactics that had accompanied his World War II exploits and early political activities, wanted to show that he could be a tough and vigorous leader. Kennedy, repeatedly relying on the so-called experts in the CIA and the military, had blundered. The American military, assuming that the president would be forced to order the intervention of United States forces once the real fighting had begun, also blundered. They seriously underestimated the president's resolve not to have American troops directly engaged in combat with the Cubans.

The intelligence reports emanating from the CIA indicating that the Cuban people would rise up against Castro also were wrong. The Cuban people failed to rise.

The next morning Castro went on Cuban television for over four hours, blaring forth his contempt for the United States and the CIA. To his credit, President Kennedy took full responsibility for the failure at the Bay of Pigs. He asked General Maxwell Taylor to undertake a complete investigation of what had gone wrong, and he directed Assistant Secretary of Defense Paul Nitze to develop a paper on Cuban-American relations from that point. Privately, however, Kennedy continued to rail against the high-level people in government who had led him astray. "My God," Kennedy said, "the bunch of advisers we inherited. . . . Can you imagine being President and leaving behind someone like all those people there?"[22]

The Bay of Pigs had serious implications that would continue to affect Cuban-American relations. Any chance that President Kennedy could somehow deal with Castro and Cuba was lost. The new American foreign policy against the island that housed a communist regime just 90 miles from the United States was to remain somewhat vague. In addition, the cold war between the United States and Russia was immediately intensified, with direct results in other areas of the world.

The burdens of office: JFK during the Bay of Pigs (The New York Times)

Within a year and a half—again in Cuba—that cold war would come close to escalating into a red-hot nuclear war.

Finally, the ultimate reaction to the Bay of Pigs came in the almost total revamping of the national security machinery. CIA director Allen Dulles was fired. Other top CIA staffers were demoted. Cuban exiles who had worked as outside contractors were no longer on the CIA payroll, and a few White House people were assigned important national security oversight duties. Richard Goodwin was given responsibility for Cuban policy and for dealing with the various exile groups. Maxwell Taylor was made the president's personal adviser on military affairs, and Robert Kennedy was always brought over for meetings that had an impact on national security.[23]

However, one thing was clear: the Kennedy presidency was off to a very poor start, even if Kennedy's popularity was still high.

Notes

1. Theodore H. White, *In Search of History* (New York, 1978), p. 496.
2. Herbert S. Parmet, *JFK: The Presidency of John F. Kennedy* (New York, 1983), pp. 62–69.
3. William L. O'Neill, *Coming Apart: An Informal History of America in the 1960's* (Chicago, 1971), p. 30.
4. Theodore Draper, *Castro's Revolution: Myths and Realities* (New York, 1962), pp. 11–12.
5. Ibid., p. 3.
6. Arthur M. Schlesinger, Jr., *A Thousand Days: John F. Kennedy in the White House* (Boston, 1965), p. 215. See also Ralph G. Martin, *A Hero for Our Time: An Intimate Story of the Kennedy Years* (New York, 1983), pp. 286–287.
7. Peter Wyden, *Bay of Pigs: The Untold Story* (New York, 1979), pp. 27–28.
8. Ibid., p. 97.
9. Ibid., p. 100. See also David Burner, *John F. Kennedy and a New Generation* (Boston, 1988), pp. 66–67.
10. Wyden, *Bay of Pigs,* p. 40 and p. 109. Rosselli and Giancana were murdered in 1975 and 1976. Both crimes remain unsolved.
11. Hugh Sidey, *John F. Kennedy, President* (New York, 1964), p. 106.
12. Schlesinger, *A Thousand Days,* pp. 239–240.
13. Ibid., p. 261. See also Wyden, *Bay of Pigs,* pp. 153–154; and quoted in Thomas C. Reeves, *A Question of Character: A Life of John F. Kennedy* (New York, 1991), pp. 264–266.
14. Quoted in Wyden, *Bay of Pigs,* pp. 156–159; and Burner, *John F. Kennedy and a New Generation,* p. 66.
15. Tad Szulc, *Fidel: A Critical Portrait* (New York, 1988), pp. 544–545.
16. Schlesinger, *A Thousand Days,* p. 269.
17. Ibid., pp. 272–273.
18. Ibid., p. 274. See also Burner, *John F. Kennedy and a New Generation,* p. 67.
19. Wyden, *Bay of Pigs,* pp. 266–272.
20. Theodore Sorensen, *Kennedy* (New York, 1965), p. 309.
21. Wyden, *Bay of Pigs,* p. 303.

22. Schlesinger, *A Thousand Days,* p. 295.
23. Ibid., p. 297.

7

THE QUEST FOR JUSTICE
JFK and Civil Rights

> "Nobody needs to convince me any
> longer that we have to solve the
> problem . . ."

In 1962, in the midst of the centennial observations of the Civil War that ended American slavery, sociologist Michael Harrington published a small book entitled *The Other America*. Harrington focused on the glaring problem that between 40 million and 50 million Americans were living in poverty. Of this group, Harrington noted, black Americans had it the worst. "Negro poverty," Harrington observed, "is unique in every way."

Part of black America's poverty problem was directly related to the fact that for a century the federal government had willfully turned its back on civil rights by allowing the segregation of blacks in virtually every aspect of American life. In education, in employment, in housing, and in transportation there were actually two Americas, one for whites and one for blacks. Harrington wrote,

> The Negro is poor because he is black . . . more importantly, the Negro is black because he is poor. The laws against color can be removed, but that will leave the poverty that is the historic and institutionalized consequence of color. As long as this is the case, being born a Negro will continue to be the most profound disability that the United States imposes upon a citizen.[1]

By 1960, when John F. Kennedy was elected to the presidency, black Americans found themselves concentrated on the lowest rung of the economic ladder of any group in the country. They had the worst and lowest-paying jobs. Of approximately 21 million black Americans, one-third lived in the rural South in poverty and terror; one-third lived in southern cities; and one-third lived in northern cities. It was a well-known fact that blacks were the last to be hired, the first to be fired and suffered the negative effects of economic recession more than others.[2]

Growing up black in the America that John F. Kennedy presided over was a painful and devastating experience. The writer Julius Lester, a teacher at the University of Massachusetts, describes what it felt like to be a young black student during that era:

> I was bewildered. . . . I had lived my then twenty-one years shuddering within the lingering shadow of slavery—segregation. I had learned to walk great distances rather than sit in the back of segregated buses, to control my bodily functions so that I would not have to use segregated bathrooms, to go for many hours without water in the southern heat rather than drink from the Colored Fountains, and to choose hunger rather than buy food from a segregated eating place. I was fourteen before I ever spoke to a white person.[3]

The prevailing myth is that President Kennedy read *The Other America* and was thus motivated to involve his administration in a full-fledged effort to change the dire condition of blacks in the United States. As a result, Kennedy has been historically linked to the evolving civil rights revolution that began in the 1950s.

The truth is, of course, far more complicated. In 1960, when Kennedy was narrowly elected to the presidency, he carried the heart of the Old South. North Carolina, South Carolina, Georgia, Alabama, Mississippi, Louisiana, Arkansas and Texas all fell into the ranks of the triumphant Democrats.[4]

Southern Democrats held the highest positions of leadership and controlled the most important committees in Congress. As a senator, Kennedy had even voted with his southern counterparts to place an amendment into the Civil Rights Act of 1957 that guaranteed a jury trial to anyone accused of violating the civil rights of blacks. Of course, that would automatically guarantee acquittal, since juries in the South during this period were made up almost exclusively of whites. Blacks were denied the vote, a basic right of citizenship. As a result they were, in most cases, excluded from serving on juries.

Although black Americans voted heavily for John F. Kennedy in 1960, the reality is that he did not have to promise much to get their vote. And, as president, he was not initially concerned with the plight of black America. His 1960 campaign had operated on the basic assumption that black voters in the North could be reached on election day by their key political leaders—the powerful black political bosses in the major cities, such as Congressman Adam Clayton Powell in New York and Congressman William Dawson in Chicago.[5]

Aside from some servants and custodial staff, the Kennedy White House had no blacks who could influence the president's thinking. The administration was far more concerned with global issues and with the Soviet threat than it was with civil rights. As Martin Luther King, Jr., the most important national leader in the fight for civil rights, said, "He [Kennedy] didn't quite have the emotional commitment . . . the moral passion is missing."[6] Thus it fell to Robert Kennedy and the Justice Department to take the initiative in the struggle for civil rights and to advance the Kennedy administration's thrust for equal rights.

When Robert Kennedy was made attorney general the new administration had generated its first controversy. How could the president have chosen his own brother for such an important job? The president-elect's answer was to the point: "I need him," John F. Kennedy said.[7] The *New York Times* editorialized, "The one appointment thus far that we find most disappointing is Mr. Kennedy's choice of younger brother Robert Kennedy as Attorney General." Even Yale University law professor Alexander Bickel, a constitutional scholar, wrote that Robert Kennedy was not fit to be attorney general (though he must have changed his mind about him, because in 1968 Bickel campaigned for Robert Kennedy for president). In the course of time, Kennedy would prove his critics wrong—especially in the crucial area of civil rights.[8]

Like his brother, the new 35-year-old attorney general had written a well-known book—*The Enemy Within,* about organ-

ized crime in the United States. But Robert F. Kennedy was
hardly an intellectual; he had graduated 56th in a class of 123
at the University of Virginia Law School. Kennedy, in fact, held
few firm ideological beliefs as a young man. With his high-
pitched voice, he was not a great speaker, and he always looked
somewhat rumpled working in his shirtsleeves. But Robert
Kennedy was tough, loyal to a fault and, unlike his brother the
president, he often saw social problems in terms of the human
beings who were most seriously affected. As attorney general,
Kennedy would be a tireless worker, putting in long hours at
the Justice Department.[9]

Robert Kennedy's biggest problem within the administration
came from a supposed subordinate, J. Edgar Hoover, the head
of the Federal Bureau of Investigation (FBI). The authoritar-
ian Hoover quickly grew to dislike the Kennedys. He was
especially unhappy with Robert Kennedy's independent and
unorthodox style of running the Justice Department.

Hoover's power in the government was broad and deep.
Although Robert Kennedy had the White House and the power
of the presidency behind him, Hoover had the whole FBI—a
vast national police force he could control like a dictator and
utilize in any way he chose.

J. Edgar Hoover had enjoyed a good relationship with the
Kennedys. He had been a longtime personal friend of Joseph
Kennedy and had even cooperated in the 1950s when Robert
Kennedy had been investigating racketeers for the Senate. In
1960, Hoover did not object to the appointment of Robert
Kennedy as attorney general even though he had supported
Richard Nixon for president. He initially thought he would be
able to control both Kennedy brothers. He had even sent Robert
Kennedy a note of congratulations after an appearance on TV's
"Meet the Press."[10]

But there was a dark side to the Hoover-Kennedy relationship. In 1941 one of Hoover's agents had bugged one of the
many liaisons between young John F. Kennedy and the divorced Danish beauty Inga Arvad, whom the FBI suspected of
being sympathetic with the Nazis. When Kennedy became a
congressman in 1946, Hoover had already compiled a long
dossier on Kennedy's romantic exploits with attractive young
women. By the time John F. Kennedy entered the White House
in 1961, Hoover's file included movie stars like Marilyn Monroe

and Jayne Mansfield and Chicago gangster Sam Giancana's girlfriend, Judith Exner.[11]

One of the ways Hoover maintained his power in the FBI for so many years was to keep secret files on many prominent politicians. In the morally conservative years between 1924, when Hoover took over the Bureau at age 29, and the early 1960s, such damaging information deterred many a politician and president from getting rid of the sinister FBI director (although no one knew, at the time, that Hoover had a secret life of his own). The Kennedys clearly wanted to get rid of Hoover. But they were fearful that Hoover would leak his files on them—files that contained embarrassing information that was potentially so damaging that it could have cost John F. Kennedy the presidency in the next election.

J. Edgar Hoover and Robert Kennedy couldn't have seemed more different. However, in many ways they were very similar. Both were lawyers who had never practiced. Both got started in law enforcement by fighting subversion (in 1919 Hoover helped put together 60,000 dossiers on radicals and anarchists, and Kennedy had been a staffer for Senator Joseph McCarthy during McCarthy's anti-Communist crusade). Both made their reputations as staunch crime-fighters, chasing gangsters and hoodlums. Each man was obsessed with personal courage and tried to exhibit an aura of toughness. And each had his own personal demons. As one FBI official recalled,

> they were too much alike. When I looked at Bob Kennedy operating in 1961, I figured that's the way Hoover had operated in 1924 . . . same kind of temperament, impatient with inefficiency, demanding as to detail, a system of logical reasoning for a position, and pretty much of a hard taskmaster.[12]

Thus it was inevitable that they would clash. At first their differences were somewhat humorous and petty. When tourists came through FBI headquarters, the tour guides were instructed to say, "Mr. Hoover became the Director of the Bureau in 1924, the year before the attorney general was born." Robert Kennedy angrily had the line removed from the official brochure and from the tour.

For his part, Hoover was horrified by the strange ways of the new intruders into his kingdom. He didn't like their casual dress and attitude. Often the attorney general would bring his beloved Brumus, an overgrown Labrador retriever, to the Justice Department, where dogs were strictly forbidden. The big dog would roam at will through the corridors of the Justice Department and would often soil the luxurious carpets, which the director of the FBI found especially offensive. But what bothered Hoover the most was the fact that Kennedy often contacted his FBI agents directly, without going through or alerting Hoover. No attorney general had ever dared cross the powerful director in that fashion. Hoover saw Kennedy's practice of dropping in on FBI field offices as a deplorable invasion of his prestige, personal power and domain. Finally, Hoover no longer had the direct access to the White House that he had always enjoyed with former presidents. Since the attorney general and the president were brothers, Hoover could no longer easily go over the head of the attorney general.[13]

It was inevitable that the director of the FBI and Robert Kennedy would clash on the question of civil rights. For decades the FBI director had resisted hiring blacks as FBI agents. While no statistics exist, it was rumored that the only black

The president and the attorney general (John F. Kennedy Library)

agents in the Bureau served in menial tasks, as drivers or office clerks. Although Hoover had been forced to accept more blacks as agents, by 1964 there were only 28 black agents. Hoover, an unabashed racist, staunchly opposed the growing civil rights struggle and was convinced that the movement and many of its key leaders were inspired, if not controlled, by the Communist Party.[14]

The modern civil rights movement began in 1955 in Montgomery, Alabama when Rosa Parks, a black seamstress, had refused to give up her seat on a late afternoon bus to a white. Blacks were forced to ride in the back of the bus or had to give up their seats to whites if a bus was overcrowded. Parks was arrested, and the black community responded by uniting behind a boycott of the citywide transportation system. The Montgomery bus boycott had sprung full-blown from the power of the black churches in that community. When the black church leaders flexed their muscle for almost a year, the white community of Montgomery ultimately, out of economic necessity, was forced to pay attention. Of the many church leaders who came together in Montgomery, the media focused its attention on one leader, Dr. Martin Luther King, Jr., the pastor of the Dexter Avenue Baptist Church.

King, who had received his Ph.D. in theology from Boston University, was a philosophical disciple of Gandhi, Thoreau and the Bible. Like the great Indian leader Gandhi, he preached a philosophy of nonviolence—the Christian principle of turning the other cheek to your enemies. King believed strongly that the tactical way to meet the ongoing hatred against blacks in American society was with nonviolence.

The white South was slow to understand the moral superiority that was implicit in Dr. King's powerful message. Thus, at the outset, they met nonviolent marches and demonstrations with violent force and brutality. As King had predicted, the civil rights movement was strengthened. The outside world grew increasingly uncomfortable watching the white South respond to the civil rights struggle with guns, clubs and vicious dogs.[15]

The next historical step in the civil rights movement came on February 1, 1960 when four black students sat down at a whites-only lunch counter at the Woolworth's in Greensboro, North Carolina and requested service. White students at Duke

University and black students at North Carolina College soon joined forces to demand integrated service at Durham bus stations and department stores. There had been many sit-ins before. But with widespread media coverage (like John F. Kennedy, black leaders soon learned how to use television effectively), the North Carolina sit-ins captured the public's imagination, and within a few months countless other sit-ins were taking place around the South.

Then the sit-ins reached Atlanta, Georgia, where they were carefully planned and choreographed by student leaders like Julian Bond. The students begged Dr. King to come to Atlanta and give their efforts his support. King responded by coming to Atlanta and making a speech in which he called for an ongoing organization to lead the civil rights struggle; for a nationwide campaign of selective buying by black America to reward those businesses that were integrated and punish those that remained segregated; and finally, for an army of volunteers to take the movement to the streets, where, nonviolently, they would protest the inhumane conditions that a segregated American society forced on its black citizenry.[16]

For the Kennedys the civil rights crisis took on meaningful reality when James Meredith applied to "Ole Miss"—the University of Mississippi. Meredith, an eight-year veteran of the U.S. Air Force, had been a student at Jackson State College, a segregated school for blacks, when he applied to Ole Miss.

The University of Mississippi was hardly a bastion of higher learning in 1962, but it was still the best educational institution in a very poor state. Meredith, who was something of a loner and not connected in any way to the activist civil rights groups or organizations, understood clearly what the Constitution said about his rights. He was determined to exercise those rights by first qualifying and then attending the college of his choice.

By late September 1962 the university had run out of ways to legally block Meredith's enrollment. The university officials should have stated that any students who violently resisted Meredith's admission to the school would be punished. But like so many university administrators then and now, they were fearful and timid. So they said and did nothing as the day approached for Meredith to enroll at Ole Miss.

The governor of Mississippi, Ross Barnett, was caught in the middle. He had run and been elected on a strict segregationist platform that promised to keep blacks and whites segregated in Mississippi. But Barnett, though he looked like the typical racist politician from the Old South, was a realist. He knew and understood the law. What he wanted was not to be embarrassed, and to save his political face by appearing to support the continuation of segregation at Ole Miss.

In Washington, aware that a crisis was brewing on the campus, Attorney General Robert Kennedy took personal charge of the Meredith case. He secretly negotiated with Governor Barnett over the phone and tried to cut a deal. Barnett would be permitted to offer some token form of spoken resistance to the admission of Meredith. Then, Barnett promised Kennedy, he would step aside and permit Meredith to be admitted to the school. Kennedy, in close consultation with the president, agreed to Barnett's terms as long as the governor promised to keep order on the campus. Barnett, however, was evasive. And he was in something of a political bind. If he protected Meredith with state troops, he would look bad to the Mississippians who had elected him to office. If he didn't, Robert Kennedy could reveal the fact that they had held those secret talks. But in any case, Kennedy remained adamant. As he told Barnett, "My job is to enforce the laws of the United States—and I intend to fulfill it."

The next day when Meredith tried to register, Governor Barnett physically barred his way, and a mob surrounded the building, shouting, "Communists. . . . Go home, nigger."

A few days later, after complicated negotiations that required more than 20 phone conversations between Robert Kennedy and Governor Barnett, the governor agreed to withdraw if Kennedy would guarantee a sufficient show of federal force in the presence of U.S. marshals. But it was too late. Emotions were at a fever pitch throughout the state, and outside agitators streamed into Oxford.

On Sunday night, September 30, 1962, President Kennedy went on national television to ask Mississippians to obey the law. He said,

> If this country should ever reach the point where any man or group of men by force or threat of force could long defy

the commands of our court and our Constitution, then no law would stand free from doubt, no judge would be sure of his writ, and no citizen would be safe from his neighbors. . . . The honor of your University and State are in the balance. I am sure that the great majority of the students will uphold that honor.[17]

But as the president spoke, rioting had already broken out on campus at Ole Miss. Some 4,000 students and outsiders clashed with a small force of federal marshals. When the fighting ended, the marshals had held their ground. However, a newsman and an innocent bystander had been killed and many students were injured.

Over the next few days troops were brought onto campus, and several hundred of them actually remained until James Meredith graduated. Meredith was continually harassed, and the worst offenders were expelled by the university. The year after Meredith's admission, 39 professors who had favored integration resigned from the university. Others were forced out, including historian James Silver, who wrote about the episode in his 1964 book, *Mississippi: The Closed Society.*

Meredith eventually got his degree and went on to graduate from law school. Governor Barnett was convicted of contempt in federal court and fined. The Kennedys were happy with that result.

The Kennedy brothers came out of the incident with luster added to their image. Black Americans and their allies were now certain that the Kennedys were on the side of civil rights. As historian Herbert Parmet evaluates the events at Ole Miss,

The episode was an educational one for Jack Kennedy. He had tried to reconcile differences, to understand Barnett's political concerns, and in the end had been deceived. Politically it was not as damaging in the South as it might have been, possibly because of the speech itself or the late arrival of the troops. Kennedy came out of the affair looking like a moderate.[18]

However, black Americans would have to accommodate themselves to the slow pace of integration under the Kennedy leadership and to the painful but very real fact of life that the Kennedy administration would be unable to get a sweeping civil rights bill passed in the Congress. But, in the end, Ole Miss was finally integrated, which in and of itself was no small accomplishment in 1962. The next black student to enroll at Ole Miss was given no protection, and soon after that two more black students enrolled, as segregation in higher education in the state of Mississippi was finally laid to rest.

The incidents that more than any single series of events brought the Kennedy brothers into the civil rights struggle were the "freedom rides" that had begun in the South in the spring of 1961.

The freedom rides were organized by the Congress of Racial Equality (CORE) to test the segregated racial policies of southern bus terminals. They put the Kennedy administration in a position where it was forced to take a firm, clear and ultimately strong stand, propelled by the powerful winds of change that were blowing in the South.

On May 15, 1961, an integrated CORE group of nine volunteers was attacked near Anniston, Alabama. Their bus was burned and vandalized. On May 20 another CORE group of freedom riders was met by an angry mob of 1,000 rioters outside Montgomery, Alabama. Twenty people were injured, including John Seigenthaler, a member of Robert Kennedy's staff who had been sent to represent the White House. Hoover's FBI agents had observed the violence but had done nothing.

CORE officials quickly understood the public relations value of having nightly newscasts showing angry southern white mobs violently attacking innocent travelers, and soon over a dozen groups of freedom riders were sent throughout the Deep South. In the face of the violence directed against the CORE volunteers, the Kennedy administration did not equivocate. The Department of Justice obtained a court order from federal judge Frank Johnson, an Eisenhower appointee. The order prevented the Ku Klux Klan, the National States Rights Party (a group opposed to civil rights and integration) and the Birmingham and Montgomery police (many of whom, along with many members of local southern police forces, belonged to the Klan) from interfering with interstate travel.

In addition, Attorney General Kennedy personally intervened with the governor of Alabama and other state officials. Kennedy, after having some trouble getting in touch with

Governor John Patterson, called an official of the Greyhound Bus Company, angrily stating,

> I think you should—had better be getting in touch with Mr. Greyhound or whoever Greyhound is and somebody better give us an answer to this question. I am—the government is—going to be very much upset if this group does not get to continue their trip.[19]

Robert Kennedy also called Senator James Eastland and got the Mississippi senator to personally guarantee the safety of the riders in his state. Eastland kept his word. The Mississippi riders were not hurt. They were, however, arrested.

Afraid that continued pressure by CORE would lead to further violence, Kennedy called for a "cooling-off period." Two major newspapers, the *Washington Post* and the *New York Times,* supported the attorney general's suggestion. But black leaders were not about to let up, and even though Dr. Martin Luther King agreed to a lull, James Farmer, the militant head of CORE who had originated the idea of the freedom riders, stated, "We had been cooling off for 100 years. If we got any cooler we'd be in a deep freeze."[20]

The Kennedy Justice Department finally sent 400 federal law officers to Alabama to ensure the safety of the freedom riders. And in an unprecedented proceeding, on May 28 Attorney General Kennedy petitioned the Interstate Commerce Commission to end the segregation of interstate buses and public facilities. On November 1, 1961 the Interstate Commerce Commission banned segregation on all interstate buses and trains and in all terminals.

CORE and its white allies had won. A thousand freedom riders had finally ended almost a century of segregation in the South. CORE spent over $300,000 in legal fees alone, but with the support of the Justice Department under Robert Kennedy's leadership, the civil rights movement had prevailed. This victory only made the movement bolder, and in the end, almost every vestige of discrimination was targeted throughout the country.[21]

Civil rights leaders realized that they had a friend in Attorney General Kennedy. His office appeared to be the only important one in the administration that was deeply committed to civil rights. Kennedy was alone in his brother's administration in his close friendships with black Americans. At one famous meeting between Robert Kennedy and a number of leading black figures that included writer James Baldwin and playwright Lorraine Hansberry, the attorney general was upset and dismayed at the frustration and anger he heard.

The meeting, held at the attorney general's posh New York City apartment, opened Kennedy's eyes to black despair and fury. One young CORE worker who had been savagely beaten in the South told Kennedy that he would not fight for his country. And Hansberry, the author of the highly acclaimed play *A Raisin in the Sun,* shocked Kennedy by telling him that she would like to arm blacks so that they could shoot white people in the streets. For Kennedy, who liked meetings to have a formal and nonconfrontational agenda, this frank exchange was both a disaster and an important window through which he could view the depths of desperation in black America.[22]

It wasn't that Robert Kennedy wanted to slow the progress of civil rights. It was just that he had been schooled in a different America and, as the nation's top lawyer, he maintained strong doubts about the uses of civil disobedience. Also, as a faithful Democrat, Bob Kennedy saw the civil rights struggle in political as well as social terms. A white backlash in the South would not only tear the Democratic Party apart, it might even drive his brother from office in 1964. Thus, the attorney general and the Kennedy administration tried to turn the civil rights movement away from civil disobedience to focus on other crucial issues like voter registration in the ongoing black struggle for rights and power.

With the federal government under the leadership of John and Robert Kennedy on board the fast-moving train of civil rights, the direction was clear. After the crisis at Ole Miss the Kennedys successfully faced up to Alabama governor George Wallace, who personally tried to block black students from enrolling at the University of Alabama. Obviously, Wallace did not want the embarrassment of being arrested by federal marshals and, after an irritated President Ken-

nedy went on national television on behalf of black rights, the
university was peacefully integrated.[23]

Legislated discrimination would ultimately become part of
the American past as the civil rights movement pressed
forward. Churches would be bombed, innocent children would
be murdered, prominent leaders of both races would be assassinated and more civil rights workers would be beaten and even
killed—but the main public event of the struggle, the great
March on Washington of August 28, 1963, put the entire
nation on notice that the rights of black Americans would
have to be taken seriously and that most Americans supported full equality for all citizens.

Organized by A. Philip Randolph and Bayard Rustin, two
stalwarts of the civil rights movement, what had begun as
just another protest march ended up as a national celebration. A crowd of whites and blacks estimated to be as large
as 400,000 marched from the Washington Monument, where
they were entertained by folk singers Joan Baez and Peter,
Paul and Mary, to the Lincoln Memorial, led by the "Big Ten"
civil rights leaders locked arm-in-arm with Jewish, Catholic
and Protestant leaders. Included in the march were movie
stars and celebrities from both the Republican and Democratic
parties like Charlton Heston, Marlon Brando, Harry Belafonte
and Sidney Poitier, as well as 15 United States senators.

The message to the country was clear: the time for full
equality for all Americans was long overdue. And no one gave
that message more power or eloquence than Dr. Martin
Luther King, Jr., who enthralled the hundreds of thousands
sweltering in the steamy August heat with his magnificently
meaningful words:

> I still have a dream. It is a dream deeply rooted in the
> American dream. I have a dream that one day this nation
> will rise up and live out the true meaning of its creed—we
> hold these truths to be self-evident, that all men are created
> equal.... When we allow freedom to ring, when we let it ring
> from every village and hamlet, from every state and every
> city, we will be able to speed up that day when all of God's
> children—black men and white men, Jews and Gentiles,
> Protestants and Catholics—will be able to join hands and
> sing in the words of the old Negro spiritual, "Free at last,
> free at last; thank God Almighty, we are free at last."[24]

At first, President Kennedy and his brother Robert were opposed to the march and did their best to talk the organizers out of holding the event. But when it became clear that, no matter what the president wanted, the march would take place, Robert Kennedy urged his brother to join it rather than stand in opposition or on the sidelines. Although President Kennedy never appeared at the march, he watched the proceedings on television from the White House.

That evening President Kennedy invited a small delegation of civil rights leaders to the White House to publicly receive his blessing and support for a civil rights bill, saying, "This nation can be properly proud." Privately, the president advised the black leaders to imitate the Jews, another minority group that had been persecuted, and put their emphasis on education.[25]

In the last analysis the Kennedy administration was pulled into the struggle for civil rights. As writer Nicholas Lemann recently observed, "During his presidency, Kennedy's support for civil rights always came as the result of the black movement's prodding him into action. In civil rights leaders'

President Kennedy meets with civil rights leaders (John F. Kennedy Library)

discussions of him, words like 'cautious' and 'technical' come up again and again."[26]

Yet it was the Kennedy administration that helped to hasten the integration of state colleges in Alabama and Mississippi, presided over the desegregation of public facilities and public transportation and supported passage of an important civil rights bill that would have moved the country forward toward full rights and equality. The Kennedys, it must be recalled, did act. As journalist Hugh Sidey said, "The full weight of the national government would sooner or later be brought to bear on the problem. That was inevitable."[27]

In the end, what really mattered was perception. While John F. Kennedy certainly did not oppose the civil rights movement, he did not really see the dire condition of black America as a priority for his administration. And yet most of the American public always believed otherwise. Unlike his brother, who understood far better the impatience of black Americans, the president would have much preferred a slower and far more moderate approach to bringing about lasting institutional change in the legacy of discrimination.

John F. Kennedy's major accomplishments in civil rights always seemed calculated to give him maximum positive public exposure: the phone call to Coretta King, the integration of Ole Miss and the University of Alabama and his White House invitation to meet with the leaders of the March on Washington are examples.

But when black rioting flamed in Jackson, Mississippi following the 1963 assassination of Medgar Evers, a local NAACP leader, and spread to Savannah, Georgia, to Cambridge, Maryland, and even to New York, neither Kennedy brother seemed to comprehend that such activities sprang from depths of black poverty and despair that would eventually escalate, later in the decade, into the violent urban riots in Watts, Newark and Detroit. And it must be remembered that Robert Kennedy and the White House approved the illegal FBI wiretaps of Dr. King and his key aides, whom Hoover believed to be under Communist control.[28]

However, black Americans still viewed President Kennedy as their true champion. In mid-1963 the Louis Harris polling organization asked blacks who had done the most for Negro rights. The top three responses included the NAACP (the

National Association for the Advancement of Colored People),
Dr. Martin Luther King, Jr., and President John F. Kennedy.[29]

Notes

1. Michael Harrington, *The Other America: Poverty in the United States* (Baltimore, 1962), p. 9, p. 70 and p. 80.
2. Ibid., p. 82.
3. Peter Collier and David Horowitz, eds., *Second Thoughts: Former Radicals Look Back at the Sixties* (Lanham, Maryland, 1989), p. 213.
4. David A. Shannon, *Twentieth Century America: The United States Since the 1890's* (Chicago, 1963), p. 611.
5. Nicholas Lemann, *The Promised Land: The Great Black Migration and How It Changed America* (New York, 1992), pp. 111–112.
6. Ibid., p. 115.
7. Victor S. Navasky, *Kennedy Justice* (New York, 1971), p. xix.
8. Ibid.
9. Ibid., pp. 3–5.
10. Ibid., pp. 5–6.
11. Curt Gentry, *J. Edgar Hoover: The Man and the Secrets* (New York, 1991), pp. 469–471 and p. 493.
12. Ibid., p. 474.
13. Ibid., pp. 475–477.
14. Ibid., p. 39. See also Navasky, *Kennedy Justice,* p. 108; and Anthony Summers, *Official and Confidential: The Secret Life of J. Edgar Hoover* (New York, 1993), p. 55.
15. William L. O'Neill, *Coming Apart: An Informal History of America in the 1960's* (Chicago, 1971), p. 159. See also David L. Lewis, *King: A Critical Biography* (Baltimore, 1970), pp. 46–47.
16. Lewis, *King,* pp. 114–116.
17. O'Neill, *Coming Apart,* pp. 73–74; and quoted in Arthur M. Schlesinger, Jr., *A Thousand Days: John F. Kennedy in the White House* (Boston, 1965), pp. 942–947.
18. Herbert S. Parmet, *JFK: The Presidency of John F. Kennedy* (New York, 1983), p. 262.
19. Navasky, *Kennedy Justice,* pp. 20–21.

20. Ibid., p. 21.
21. O'Neill, *Coming Apart,* pp. 161–162.
22. Lemann, *The Promised Land,* p. 127.
23. O'Neill, *Coming Apart,* p. 162.
24. Irving Bernstein, *Promises Kept: John F. Kennedy's New Frontier* (New York, 1991), pp. 116–117.
25. Navasky, *Kennedy Justice,* p. 227. See also Schlesinger, *A Thousand Days,* p. 973; Thomas C. Reeves, *A Question of Character: A Life of John F. Kennedy* (New York, 1991), p. 359.
26. Lemann, *The Promised Land,* p. 115.
27. Hugh Sidey, *John F. Kennedy, President* (New York, 1964), p. 266.
28. Reeves, *A Question of Character,* pp. 356–357 and p. 361.
29. Schlesinger, *A Thousand Days,* p. 949.

8

ON THE BRINK
JFK and the Cuban Missile Crisis

> "Above all, while defending our own
> vital interests, nuclear powers must
> avert those confrontations which bring
> an adversary to the choice of either a
> humiliating retreat or a nuclear war."

The most dangerous moments in recent American history occurred during the crisp fall days of 1962, when the United States and Russia appeared to be on a nuclear collision course that could only have ended in great disaster for both nations. In this fearsome instance President John F. Kennedy would not only begin to prove his mettle as a leader; he would earn a place in history.

After the 1961 Bay of Pigs fiasco, relations between Cuba and the United States were practically nonexistent. Cuba and Fidel Castro had humiliated the United States and the president. Behind the scenes the CIA had been secretly plotting to get rid of Castro. Then, in October 1962, Russia once again put Cuba on the front burner for the Kennedy administration by sending nuclear missiles to the island and testing the young president's resolve.

It is still not entirely clear why Soviet Premier Nikita Khrushchev challenged Kennedy in Cuba. In June of 1961, when the president and Khrushchev met in Vienna, the Russian leader had warned Kennedy that East Germany might cut off West Berlin (Germany had been divided into East and West after World War II, with Berlin similarly divided). The cocky Soviet leader, testing his young and inexperienced counterpart, also warned Kennedy that if the United States responded with force, Russia would do the same.

Kennedy stood up to Khrushchev. The president was convinced that Berlin was the key to the successful NATO (North Atlantic Treaty Organization) alliance—a mutual assistance treaty signed in 1949 under which member nations agreed to regard an attack on one nation as an attack on all. Thus Kennedy beefed up American forces in Germany and asked Congress for an extra $3.2 billion for defense as he prepared the NATO allies for trouble. In this instance Khrushchev did nothing, and East Germans did not close off access to Berlin, although they did put up the Berlin Wall to prevent East Berliners from escaping to the West.[1]

At any rate, having appeared to have backed off from his threats over Berlin, Khrushchev was clearly testing his younger adversary in 1962 over Cuba. Of course, Fidel Castro wanted the Russian missiles. He knew that with conventional weapons Cuba could never prevent a serious American invasion. And because of his strained relations with the Kennedy administration, Castro could never be sure that such an invasion was out of the question. He believed that with a handful of missiles armed with nuclear warheads pointed at the United States, Cuba would be protected.

Whatever the reasons, Khrushchev sent the missiles. For the first time in the course of the cold war the Soviets had placed nuclear missiles in another country, and no one could explain exactly why. Later Khrushchev was to tell the Supreme Soviet,

> We carried weapons there at the request of the Cuban government. . . . These weapons were to be in the hands of Soviet military men. . . . Our aim was only to defend Cuba.[2]

But the Russian leader had badly miscalculated. First, in a democracy like the United States with a free and uncensored press, no president could hope to keep the existence of missiles in Cuba a secret for very long. Once the secret was discovered, someone in the government or the military was bound to leak it to the press. Then, once the news was made public, no administration could fail to react and hope to survive politically. To make matters worse for President Kennedy, there were the fall congressional elections facing the Democrats, and the worry of political fallout should the administration somehow repeat the mistakes of the Bay of Pigs.

In late July of 1962 the first Soviet shipments of the missile parts arrived in Cuba. Within three weeks the Central Intelligence Agency (CIA) alerted the president that "something new and different" was happening on the island. Intelligence data suggested that there were as many as 5,000 Soviet "specialists" in Cuba; that some type of military construction was going on; and that more Soviet ships were on the way, with more equipment and more Soviet technicians.

At first, the CIA and other parts of the American intelligence community concluded that the Soviets were only constructing SAM (surface-to-air missiles) sites and that the Russian goal was to bolster Castro's somewhat inadequate island defense system.[3]

But on Sunday, October 14, 1962, a U-2 spy plane, piloted by Major Rudolf Anderson, Jr., sent to photograph the missile sites, brought back chilling proof that something far more sinister was going on. The next day CIA photoanalysts concluded with certainty that the Soviet Union was in the process of installing launching sites for Soviet MRBMs (medium-range ballistic missiles) in an area 50 miles southwest of Havana. Additional photos showed that other sites were being built for intermediate missiles with a range of some 2,000 miles. The CIA's photographs clearly showed erectors and tents that could shelter 50-foot ICBMs (intercontinental ballistic missiles) as well as a storage site to receive nuclear warheads, even though there was no evidence that the ICBMs had yet arrived on the sites.[4]

Though the CIA's past record did not inspire overwhelming confidence in their analysis, in this instance the CIA's efforts were right on target. This crisis was all too real. The Russians were bent on targeting American cities with intermediate-range ballistic missiles.

President Kennedy was shown the pictures for the first time by McGeorge Bundy, his national security adviser. Bundy, who had learned of the photos 12 hours earlier, had decided to wait until morning to tell the president about them. Bundy wanted to avoid the possibility of news leaks by other members of the administration who would have been alerted, and to allow

Kennedy to have one last good night of sleep before facing the dangerous ordeal ahead.[5]

Instead of going through the national security bureaucracy and working with men who were virtual strangers to him, President Kennedy made some immediate decisions within his inner circle. First, Kennedy stated that the threat to the United States would have to be concluded by removing the missiles. Second, the president instructed Bundy to immediately begin low-level photographic flights over Cuba and to set up an emergency meeting of top officials. As for Kennedy personally, Arthur Schlesinger, Jr. recalled, "Privately he was furious: if Khrushchev could pull this after all his protestations and denials, how could he ever be trusted on anything?"[6]

Above everything, President Kennedy insisted on strict secrecy. McGeorge Bundy remembers that the president wanted "extraordinary precautions" taken in order to prevent leaks that might lead the Soviets to second-guess the American resolve and miscalculate, with the catastrophic result of atomic war. Bundy writes,

> the immediate danger . . . was not from Russian spies but from American newsmen who fortunately for us, did not know the race [against the story becoming public] was on.[7]

Kennedy also created what came to be known as ExComm— short for the Executive Committee of the National Security Council. This group of men met on and off for the better part of the next few weeks to deal with the crisis. ExComm included Vice President Lyndon B. Johnson, Attorney General Robert Kennedy, and cabinet secretaries Dean Rusk (State), Douglas Dillon (Treasury) and Robert McNamara (Defense). Other key presidential advisers on ExComm included George Ball (whose conference room at the State Department was where the group met), McGeorge Bundy, Ted Sorensen, Ambassador Charles Bohlen, General Maxwell Taylor, and new CIA director John McCone. Other experts like Roswell Gilpatric and former secretary of state Dean Acheson were brought into meetings as needed, and United Nations ambassador Adlai Stevenson joined when he could get away from New York without overly arousing media suspicions that something was seriously wrong in Washington.

These men were trusted by Kennedy in a way that he could not trust others in the government. At the first meeting Kennedy was hardly in his usual jocular frame of mind. Aides recall that his words were carefully chosen and that he appeared "very clipped, very tense." Kennedy told the group that he believed that the Russians meant business and that the United States was involved in the most serious international crisis he had yet faced. Marine commandant General David M. Shoup summed up the group's feelings when he said, "You are in a pretty bad fix, Mr. President." In the one light moment during the meeting, President Kennedy stared back at his general and said, "You are in it with me."[8]

The Joint Chiefs of Staff had a simple solution to the crisis: bomb the missile sites or invade the island. Led by Air Force general Curtis LeMay, these military men argued that a strategic preemptive attack was essential. They assured the president that the Russians would not respond. But the president was skeptical about what the Russians might do. Robert Kennedy recalled his brother saying,

> They, no more than we, can let these things go by without doing something. They can't, after all their statements, permit us to take out their missiles, kill a lot of Russians, and then do nothing. If they don't take action in Cuba, they certainly will in Berlin.[9]

After the first few meetings, President Kennedy turned the chairmanship over to his brother Robert so that he could fulfill previous commitments. To avoid arousing unnecessary suspicion, Kennedy was determined not to alter his public schedule. But, more important, Kennedy soon learned that his absence from ExComm was an asset, in that it encouraged members of the group to speak more freely. The president hoped to avoid some of the consensus thinking that had characterized White House discussions during the Bay of Pigs.

One member of the Joint Chiefs, a military hawk, even suggested a nuclear strike, which could have meant the deaths of hundreds of thousands of Cubans. But Robert Kennedy sided with Secretary of Defense Robert McNamara, who argued forcefully in favor of a military blockade around Cuba. Kennedy later recalled, "I could not accept the idea that the United

States would rain bombs on Cuba, killing thousands and thousands of civilians in a surprise attack."

The idea of nuclear war horrified the Kennedys as they listened to their chief military advisers speak coolly and confidently of the American capacity to devastate Cuba. As he weighed the arguments favoring a nuclear response, Robert Kennedy said,

> I thought, as I listened, of the many times that I had heard the military take positions which, if wrong, had the advantage that no one would be around at the end to know.[10]

Listening to a discussion of an air strike against the missile sites, Robert Kennedy passed a note to Theodore Sorensen that said, "I now know how Tojo felt when he was planning Pearl Harbor." (Tojo was the prime minister of Japan who decided on the surprise attack against the United States at Pearl Harbor in 1941.)[11]

While people's positions changed throughout the debate, Robert Kennedy remained surprisingly moderate and practical. As the key figure on ExComm after the president (although Robert Kennedy's role and importance have been disputed by some ExComm members like former secretary of state Dean Rusk[12]), he was the one member of the group who did not have to worry about losing his job, and was ultimately the person most responsible for the nonviolent and successful resolution of the Cuban missile crisis.

The momentousness of the situation was never lost on Robert Kennedy, who realized that the strain, after hours of sleeplessness and endless meetings, was beginning to show on his ExComm colleagues. Kennedy said, "Each one of us was being asked to make a recommendation which, if wrong and if accepted, could mean the destruction of the human race."[13]

On Thursday morning, October 18, President Kennedy called ExComm to the cabinet room at the White House. Theodore Sorensen reported that Secretary of State Dean Rusk had proposed an immediate "'surgical' air strike without warning." But this was opposed by the diplomats on the team, who were opting for the president to take "prior political action," which meant somehow negotiating with Khrushchev.[14]

It would have been easy to give Russia a private warning, because Russian foreign minister Andrei Gromyko was scheduled to meet with the president that day. But then two more dangers would have cropped up for Kennedy: the Americans would alert Russia to the fact that they knew what was going on, which meant that should the military strike option become inevitable, the Russians would have had more time to prepare; and any secret negotiations always ran the risk of exposure by the media before matters could be settled. And this, with the congressional elections looming, was a recipe for political disaster.

Meanwhile, the military men seemed united in their opposition to a limited air strike. Still smarting from the drubbing of the Bay of Pigs, the Joint Chiefs argued that if military force was to be used, this time their hands must not be tied. The president was, of course, keenly aware of how disgruntled the military had become after the Bay of Pigs, and he repeatedly put tough questions to the Joint Chiefs.

What President Kennedy wanted from his advisers was a clear consensus—a unanimity of opinion on what was to be done. What he seemed to be getting was a multiplicity of opinions and options that only increased the confusion. Late that night, weary of the endless posturing, pontificating and debating that characterized the ExComm meetings, the president told his advisers, "Whatever you fellows are recommending today, you will be sorry about a week from now."[15]

To further complicate matters, the president and ExComm were now in a race against the clock. An examination of new aerial surveillance photos taken on October 17 revealed that several more installations, which could house between 16 and 32 missiles with a range of over 1,000 miles, had been constructed. American military experts estimated that the missiles would be operational within a week, and by October 18 intelligence estimates revealed that at least half of the Soviet Union's entire atomic warhead ICBM potential, made up of intermediate-range ballistic missiles directed against American cities, would soon be in Cuba. CIA estimates presented a chilling picture to President Kennedy and his advisers: within a few minutes after these atomic missiles were fired, eighty million Americans would be dead.[16]

Gradually, the members of ExComm began to move toward the McNamara position advocating a naval blockade. Robert Kennedy revealed that President Kennedy favored a blockade against the Soviets because it would allow the world to see that the United States was not the aggressor and, at the same time, would toss the ball back in Khrushchev's court—the choice to run the blockade would be his.

Meanwhile, President Kennedy gave instructions to the military to prepare for the worst. American Strategic Air Command bombers loaded with a nuclear payroll were put on full alert and began circling the earth. The First Armored Division, consisting of 15,000 infantrymen and four tank battalions, was ordered to the East Coast to prepare for an invasion by Cuba. American civilians were evacuated from the U.S. naval base at Guantanamo on the Cuban coast, and Secretary of Defense McNamara ordered four tactical squadrons to be placed at readiness for possible air strikes against the island. The navy prepared a fleet of 180 vessels, and the army readied 250,000 troops for an invasion of Cuba if one became necessary. And Polaris submarines, armed with nuclear warheads, began heading for the Soviet Union as the most dangerous showdown of the cold war moved toward an uncertain conclusion. Only one thing was clear: President Kennedy's rearmament program was already producing a massive dividend, since such a flexible and rapid military response had not been available during the Eisenhower years.[17]

Throughout the ExComm deliberations the president had managed to maintain his busy schedule, while simultaneously remaining up to date on the crisis. He had stopped in Springfield, Illinois to lay a wreath on Lincoln's grave. Then it was off to Chicago to campaign for Democratic congressional candidates and to give a speech before Mayor Daley's Cook County Democrats.

On Saturday, October 20, the president received a call from his brother at 10 A.M. in Chicago. The time had come, with U.S. forces on the alert and in place, Bob Kennedy told the president, for a decision. A presidential speech to the nation was scheduled for Sunday night.

President Kennedy instructed his press secretary, Pierre Salinger, to tell the press that he had developed a cold, and after calling his wife to tell her that he wanted her and the children close by, he flew back to Washington. That afternoon Kennedy presided over ExComm for the final meeting. Once again McNamara set out the case for a military blockade of Cuba, and for one final time the military men, with some civilian support, made a plea for a Pearl Harbor–like strike. A straw vote was taken, with 11 members voting for a blockade (or a "quarantine," as ExComm preferred to term the action) and six voting for a military strike. Then Kennedy issued orders to prepare for the "quarantine" option.[18]

On October 21 President Kennedy attended mass and arrived at the White House before 11 A.M. He met that afternoon with his National Security Council to discuss informing America's allies. That evening he met with Vice President Johnson, who had been briefed by McGeorge Bundy. The president and the vice president reviewed the international situation to determine how the crisis would affect world politics. Meanwhile, Ted Sorensen worked on the speech that Kennedy would give to the nation—now rescheduled for Monday night.

On October 22 Kennedy informed his cabinet and a delegation of congressional leaders of the decision. The congressional leaders, especially Senators Richard B. Russell of Georgia and J. William Fulbright of Arkansas, irritated Kennedy by advising military action instead of approving of the blockade. As Robert Kennedy wrote, "The President, after listening to the frequently emotional criticism, explained that he would take whatever steps were necessary to protect the security of the United States, but that he did not feel greater military action was warranted initially."[19]

At six o'clock the president met with Soviet ambassador Anatoly Dobrynin and ordered the surprised diplomat to instruct his country to remove the missiles from Cuba. Then, at precisely 7 P.M., President Kennedy set forth the situation to the American people in a nationally televised address. With a grave expression and in a firm voice Kennedy told the American people all that he had known since October 16th. "The purpose of these bases," Kennedy said somberly, "can be none other than to provide a nuclear strike capability against the Western Hemisphere."[20]

The president pulled no punches. He said that the American people had been deliberately deceived by the Soviets and could not stand for it. Thus, Kennedy told the world, he would run any risk, including thermonuclear war, in order to safeguard and protect the interests of the United States. Then he outlined his initial plans: a quarantine on all offensive military equipment being shipped to Cuba; intensified surveillance of Cuba itself; a declaration that any nuclear missile launched from Cuba against any nation in the Western Hemisphere would be considered an attack by the Soviet Union on the United States; reinforcement of the American base at Guantanamo; an immediate convening of the Organization of American States to consider the threat; and an emergency meeting of the United Nations Security Council to consider the threat to world peace. Finally, Kennedy appealed to Khrushchev himself "to halt and eliminate this clandestine, reckless and provocative threat to world peace and to stable relations between our two nations."[21]

For the first time in American history a world crisis was brought live into the living rooms of the American people by their president. As he had done in his TV debates with Richard Nixon during the campaign, John F. Kennedy was changing the rules and ushering in a new age of political communication. After Kennedy's address, TV newsmen appeared with large maps showing that every American city but Seattle was within range of the Russian missiles. As one scholar of Kennedy's speech has noted,

> It represented a landmark in political communication for it was the first time a president had used television in quite this way. . . . Its impact was extraordinary. Over the ensuing days, the entire nation followed the unfolding crisis which Kennedy had sprung upon it with such drama.[22]

Each day the tension grew as TV coverage of the Cuban missile crisis flashed across the small screens of America. The networks issued regular news bulletins in addition to news specials and updates as the Russian ships approached the blockade line where American naval warships were ordered to stop them by force.

Life across the United States, however, did not come to a total screeching halt. Most Americans went on with their lives as usual although, in some cities and towns, schoolchildren began to practice hiding under their desks and covering their heads

in preparation for a nuclear attack. No American co‿
thinking about the approaching Russian ships. Would they ‿
to cross the blockade or fire on the Americans? Would they be
sunk? Would the Russians retaliate? If so, how would the
United States respond? More than a few American citizens
slept uneasily during those long nights of uncertainty.

For the most part, the American people supported the Kennedy decision to blockade the Russian missile shipments to
Cuba. Years and years of anti-Soviet cold war indoctrination
had taken root in the American mind. The Russians were the
bad guys; the Americans were the good guys. Some people even
argued that massive atomic destruction was preferable to
allowing the Russians to do in Cuba exactly what the United
States had already done in Turkey (U.S. missiles armed with
nuclear warheads were pointed at the Soviet Union from
launching sites along the Russian border in Turkey).

The one journalist to openly oppose Kennedy's decision-making was the syndicated columnist Walter Lippmann. He questioned the decision to resort to direct confrontation with the
Russians without trying to resolve the situation diplomatically. But the columnist James Reston of the *New York Times*
countered Lippmann by suggesting that Khrushchev had gambled in Cuba to make a deal to get U.S. missiles out of Turkey.
Reston had nothing but praise for Kennedy, writing that the
president was faced with a "power play" and that he had
"reduced the dangers of miscalculation in Moscow by demonstrating his willingness to fight for the vital interests of the
United States."[23]

U Thant, the secretary general of the United Nations, urged
the superpowers to walk away from one another for a few weeks
so that things might calm down. But President Kennedy never
even considered this option. Kennedy had made his decision:
the Soviet Union would either back down by accepting the
American blockade and removing the offensive missiles, or face
nuclear destruction.

On October 24 the crisis appeared to abate when the Soviets
diverted or halted a dozen ships on their way to Cuba. But that
did not mean the crisis was over, even though Secretary of
State Dean Rusk exclaimed, "We're eyeball to eyeball and I
think the other fellow just blinked."[24]

Then, on October 26, the Soviet-chartered ship *Marucla* was stopped and boarded by order of the president. Since the ship was owned by Panama, President Kennedy was giving Khrushchev some leeway. As Robert Kennedy said,

> He was demonstrating to Khrushchev that we were going to enforce the quarantine and yet, because it was not a Soviet-owned vessel, it did not represent a direct affront to the Soviets requiring a response from them. It gave them more time, but simultaneously demonstrated that the U.S. meant business.[25]

At the same time, Khrushchev appeared to be looking for a way out of the crisis. In a long and emotional letter, teletyped to Kennedy by the American embassy in Moscow, the Soviet chairman insisted that while the missiles were for defensive purposes only, he did not expect the president to believe him. Therefore, Khrushchev implied that in return for a pledge by the president not to invade Cuba, he would withdraw the missiles. The next day another letter arrived from Khrushchev. This letter was much tougher, and stated that the Russians would remove their missiles only if the United States removed its missiles from Turkey.

Kennedy had liked Khrushchev's first suggestion, but his ExComm advisers warned him of a Russian trick, and again began speaking of invading Cuba and of air strikes. Secretary of State Dean Rusk saw the first Khrushchev letter as vague and without a firm commitment to pull out the missiles or a way to verify that the missiles had indeed been pulled out.[26]

Then, in a masterstroke of international strategy, Robert Kennedy suggested that the president respond to Khrushchev's first letter while ignoring the second. On October 27 President Kennedy wrote Khrushchev, "I have read your letter of October 26th with great care and welcomed the statement of your desire to seek a prompt solution." Kennedy went on to inform the chairman that as soon as the Soviets stopped work on the missile bases and rendered the warheads inoperable under United Nations supervision, he would be ready to negotiate the settlement that Khrushchev had suggested. In addition, Kennedy vaguely alluded to a solution to the problem of the U.S. bases and missiles in Turkey.[27]

Kennedy sent the letter accepting Khrushchev's implied proposal through the Russian ambassador, Anatoly Dobrynin, and instructed the ambassador that if no reply was received in two to three days, Cuba would be bombed. Clearly, Kennedy was playing tough.

The Kennedy strategy worked, and on October 28 Radio Moscow announced that the Cuban missile sites were being dismantled.

President Kennedy and his brother Robert had skillfully faced the Russians down. In the aftermath of the crisis, however, some observers wondered whether it had been necessary to go to the very brink of nuclear war to resolve the situation. The respected writer I. F. Stone argued that the risk of nuclear devastation seemed disproportionate to the threat posed by the Russians, and wondered whether such a close call would have been worth it if events had gone the other way. Stone wrote,

> When a whole people is in a state of mind where it is ready to risk extinction—its own and everybody else's—as a means of having its own way in an international dispute, the readiness for murder has become a way of life and a world menace.[28]

However, most contemporary observers and scholars gave John F. Kennedy high marks. Kennedy aide Arthur M. Schlesinger, Jr. felt that Kennedy had acted wisely and magnificently. He wrote,

> It was this combination of toughness and restraint, of will, nerve and wisdom, so brilliantly controlled, so matchlessly calibrated, that dazzled the world. Before the missile crisis people might have feared that we would use our power extravagantly or not use it at all. But the thirteen days gave the world—even the Soviet Union—a sense of American determination and responsibility in the use of power which, if sustained, might indeed become a turning point in the history of relations between east and west.[29]

President Kennedy himself realized that perhaps things had gotten somewhat out of hand, and hoped that in the future nations with such awesome weapons of mass destruction would be much more careful. Kennedy said, "Above all,

The opponents in the Cuban missile crisis of October 1962: President Kennedy and Soviet Premier Nikita Khrushchev (John F. Kennedy Library)

while defending our own vital interests, nuclear powers must avert those confrontations which bring an adversary to the choice of either a humiliating retreat or a nuclear war."[30]

The Cuban missile crisis was the major success of the Kennedy presidency. President Kennedy had demonstrated to the

Russians and to the world that he was capable of responding calmly and boldly to crisis. It also enabled the president to finally enter into serious negotiations with the Russians that ultimately led to the nuclear test-ban treaty. Before the world hovered on the edge of nuclear disaster in the missile crisis, this would have been impossible. But now, both Russia and the United States clearly realized the dangers of the atomic age and how, by lessening cold war tensions, the world could become a much safer place.

For Nikita Khrushchev the missile crisis was a disaster—a Bay of Pigs in reverse. In Russia Khrushchev found himself severely criticized for what his critics called "adventurism" and for failing to stand up to Kennedy in the crisis. Within two years Khrushchev was ruined. In 1964 he fell from power and was replaced by a series of tougher and far more sinister leaders.

Finally, the Cuban missile crisis helped to define the limits of American power in the nuclear age. It was clear that the military men who had argued for a nuclear strike had been wrong. The United States could not resort to nuclear force in any situation, whether it was in Cuba, Germany or Vietnam. To do so would have been suicidal for the American people, because it was clear that no winner could emerge from any nuclear confrontation, with its prospect of casualties numbering in the tens of millions.

Thus the Kennedy administration had resisted the incredible Dr. Strangelove types on ExComm who initially argued for bombing Cuba and who insisted that some sort of victory could actually be gained in a nuclear exchange with the Soviet Union. Of course, there were many in government and in the armed services who still argued that traditional military force was a practical possibility—especially in dealing with the spread of Soviet-style communism in the underdeveloped nations of the Third World, where it seemed that the growth of democratic government was more threatened than ever.

And that theory was put to the test in Southeast Asia as President John F. Kennedy decided to involve the United States more deeply in the war against communism in South Vietnam. Sadly, as Americans were eventually to find out at great cost, conventional military strategies were also to become a major casualty of the cold war thinking that led to the greatest misadventure in the post–World War II era for the United States: John F. Kennedy's greatest mistake, the involvement of the United States in the expanding war in Vietnam.

Notes

1. Irving Bernstein, *Promises Kept: John F. Kennedy's New Frontier* (New York, 1991), p. 290. See also Peter Wyden, *Wall: The Inside Story of Divided Berlin* (New York, 1989).
2. Arthur M. Schlesinger, Jr., *A Thousand Days: John F. Kennedy in the White House* (Boston, 1965), pp. 795–796. See also McGeorge Bundy, *Danger and Survival: Choices About the Bomb in the First Fifty Years* (New York, 1988), pp. 415–427 on "Khrushchev's Reasons and Why We Missed Them."
3. Schlesinger, *A Thousand Days,* pp. 797–798.
4. Herbert S. Parmet, *JFK: The Presidency of John F. Kennedy* (New York, 1983), p. 284.
5. Bundy, *Danger and Survival,* pp. 395–396.
6. Schlesinger, *A Thousand Days,* p. 802.
7. Bundy, *Danger and Survival,* p. 396.
8. Parmet, *JFK,* p. 285; and quoted in Robert F. Kennedy, *Thirteen Days: A Memoir of the Cuban Missile Crisis* (New York, 1969), pp. 36–37.
9. Kennedy, *Thirteen Days,* p. 36.
10. Ibid., p. 37 and p. 48.
11. Ibid., p. 41 and p. 44; and quoted in Michael R. Beschloss, *The Crisis Years: Kennedy and Khrushchev 1960–1963* (New York, 1991), p. 435. RFK and Sorensen remember the note passing differently. RFK claims he gave the note to the president.
12. Beschloss, *The Crisis Years,* p. 452.
13. Kennedy, *Thirteen Days,* p. 44.
14. Beschloss, *The Crisis Years,* p. 453.
15. Parmet, *JFK,* p. 286.
16. Kennedy, *Thirteen Days,* pp. 35–36.
17. Parmet, *JFK,* p. 287. See also William L. O'Neill, *Coming Apart: An Informal History of America in the 1960's* (Chicago, 1971), p. 69.

18. Schlesinger, *A Thousand Days,* p. 808. See also Parmet, *JFK,* p. 288.
19. Kennedy, *Thirteen Days,* pp. 53–54.
20. Schlesinger, *A Thousand Days,* p. 808.
21. Kennedy, *Thirteen Days,* pp. 135–137.
22. Mary Ann Watson, *The Expanding Vista: American Television in the Kennedy Years* (New York, 1990), pp. 78–79.
23. Montague Kern, Patricia W. Levering and Ralph B. Levering, *The Kennedy Crises: The Press, the Presidency, and Foreign Policy* (Chapel Hill, North Carolina, 1983), pp. 129–130.
24. O'Neill, *Coming Apart,* pp. 69–70.
25. Kennedy, *Thirteen Days,* p. 82.
26. Ralph G. Martin, *A Hero for Our Time: An Intimate Story of the Kennedy Years* (New York, 1983), p. 415. See also Beschloss, *The Crisis Years,* p. 523.
27. Schlesinger, *A Thousand Days,* p. 829.
28. O'Neill, *Coming Apart,* p. 71.
29. Schlesinger, *A Thousand Days,* p. 841. For a complete contemporary analysis of the Cuban missile crisis by participants and by Russian and American scholars, see James G. Blight and David A. Welch, *On the Brink: Americans and Soviets Reexamine the Cuban Missile Crisis* (New York, 1990).
30. O'Neill, *Coming Apart,* p. 71.

9

THE LEGACY
JFK and Vietnam

"I'm going to be very firm about not
committing myself or this country or its
troops to a situation we can't win . . ."

On January 19, 1961, on the day before the inauguration,
the president-elect met with President Dwight Eisenhower. They were meeting for only the second time since
the election, and had not met once in Kennedy's eight years as
a United States senator.

Eisenhower warned Kennedy of some of the dangers he
would face in the field of American foreign policy. In part,
Eisenhower said,

> If Laos falls to the Communists, then it would be a question
> of time until South Vietnam, Cambodia, Thailand and
> Burma would collapse. . . . This is one of the problems I'm
> leaving you that I'm not happy about. We may have to
> fight.[1]

As a congressman in the 1940s and early 1950s John F.
Kennedy was only vaguely aware of the problem in Vietnam,
which was known in those days as French Indochina because
France had colonized the country in the 19th century. After
World War II, with the Japanese who had taken over Indochina
defeated, France again tried to reassert its control in the
region. The French colonialists were opposed by Ho Chi Minh,
a Vietnamese nationalist who was also a Communist. Ho had

seized Hanoi, the capital city of the North, in 1945, and had declared the independent state of the Democratic Republic of Vietnam. The French soon began an attempt to restore control.

Initially, the United States took little interest in the struggle between the French and the insurgent Vietnamese. But as the French situation worsened, the United States found itself more deeply embroiled in the cold war with the Soviet Union and Communist China. Thus, in the late 1940s and early 1950s, the Truman administration found itself supporting the French to the tune of about 40% of the war's cost after the State Department had recommended that "all practicable measures be taken to prevent further Communist expansion in Southeast Asia."[2]

After a visit to Vietnam in 1951, John F. Kennedy argued against aiding the French. In 1954 Senator Kennedy warned that Vietnam was a dangerous place in which to get bogged down in a war. He saw, he said, "an enemy which is everywhere and at the same time nowhere, 'an enemy of the people' which has the sympathy and covert support of the people."[3]

By the time the French were finally defeated at the battle of Dienbienphu in 1954, the United States was footing 80% of the cost of the conflict. At the peace conference, the Eisenhower administration managed to get Indochina divided into four parts: Laos and Cambodia became independent, and Vietnam was partitioned into North and South Vietnam, with the northern half controlled from Hanoi by the Communists under Ho Chi Minh and the southern portion ruled from Saigon as the Republic of Vietnam. It was also agreed that a free national election would be held in 1956.

The anticommunist leader of South Vietnam, Premier Ngo Dinh Diem, was not politically strong enough to win a national election against his enemy Ho Chi Minh. Ho was seen by many of the people, especially the peasants, as the father of Vietnamese independence. So Diem refused to hold the elections that had been promised to unify the divided country.

With American aid, Diem was strong enough to rule from Saigon and to fight the Communists, who by 1960 had organized the National Liberation Front (NLF), called the Viet Cong by the Americans.[4]

During the late 1950s Senator Kennedy's views changed. He came to see Vietnam as vital to American interests in Southeast Asia. In 1956 Senator Kennedy expressed that change, saying,

> Vietnam represents the cornerstone of the Free World in Southeast Asia, the keystone to the arch, the finger in the dike. . . . Her economy is essential to the economy of all of Southeast Asia.[5]

When he became president, John F. Kennedy's changed views on Vietnam were immediately apparent. "This is the worst one we've got, isn't it?" Kennedy asked his aide Walter Rostow only six days after his inauguration. Rostow, President Kennedy's specialist on Southeast Asia on the National Security Council, had given Kennedy a report on Vietnam written by Edward Lansdale, a master in covert operations and a recognized expert on Vietnam. "You know," Kennedy continued, "Eisenhower never mentioned it. He talked at length about Laos, but never uttered the word Vietnam."[6]

Like President Eisenhower before him, John F. Kennedy had been schooled in the rabid anticommunism of the cold war world. From Woodrow Wilson's time on, American presidents had been constantly grappling with an increasingly global foreign policy. If the United States stood for democracy, how could Americans turn their backs on a troubled world? And, like Eisenhower, Kennedy believed in the "domino theory" that said that if one country fell to communism, its neighbors, like falling dominoes, would soon follow. As Kennedy stated,

> I believe it. China is so large, looms so high just beyond the frontiers, that [South Vietnam's fall] would not only give an improved geographic position for guerrilla assault on Malaya, but . . . also give the impression that the wave of the future in Southeast Asia was China and the Communists.[7]

On March 15, 1961, President Kennedy replaced Ambassador Elbridge Durbrow with Frederick E. Nolting, Jr. Nolting was a steadfast supporter of the Diem regime.

During Durbrow's time in Vietnam, the Viet Cong (Vietnamese Communists) had expanded their operations to the point that in some areas of the South they had become the effective government. The Viet Cong were supported and controlled by military advisers from Hanoi. But most of their support came from native southerners who had returned to South Vietnam.[8]

The Viet Cong program was simple. To win the hearts and minds of the largely peasant population in the distant villages of the countryside, they murdered uncooperative leaders, and they offered land to the peasants and some autonomy to the non-Vietnamese tribes who inhabited the mountainous and remote regions of the country. The energy, brutality and dedication of the Viet Cong was in stark contrast to the arrogant and corrupt government officials who supported the Diem regime.[9]

To make matters worse, Diem had alienated the Buddhists who made up the majority of South Vietnam's population. Since 1954 Diem had always given the Catholics preferential treatment. When one million predominately Catholic refugees fled the North, Diem not only welcomed them with open arms, he saw their return as a chance to insert fellow Catholics into key governmental and military positions in the country. In addition, the Catholic Church enjoyed a special legal status under Diem's rule.

In May of 1963, when the Buddhists held a festival, Diem's brother, the archbishop of Hue, ordered that religious flags not be flown. The Buddhists defied the order and refused to disperse during a rally. The Catholic deputy province chief ordered his troops to fire on the crowd, and seven people, including two children, were killed.[10]

Soon Americans were seeing shocking images on TV newscasts of Buddhist monks dousing themselves with gasoline, setting themselves on fire and burning to death as a protest against the Diem regime. It did not help matters when President Diem's sister-in-law, Madame Nhu, the wife of Diem's unscrupulous brother Ngo Dinh Nhu, described the Buddhist suicides as a "barbecue" and said that if the Buddhists wanted to burn themselves alive, "I will be glad to supply the gasoline. Let them burn and we shall clap our hands."[11]

By 1962 the Kennedy administration was clearly disregarding the hard realities of the situation. The political survival of South Vietnam became a priority in American planning for the entire region.

The irony is that Kennedy totally ignored the warning of French president Charles DeGaulle, who had seen his own country defeated by the Communists in Vietnam and who wrote, "I predict that you will sink step by step into a bottomless military and political quagmire, however much you spend in men and money."[12]

In the spring of 1961, after a trip to South Vietnam, Vice President Lyndon Johnson reported a situation in which Viet Cong troop strength had increased from 4,000 to 16,000. President Kennedy was clearly alarmed by Johnson's report.

In late 1961, after a visit to Vietnam, General Maxwell Taylor and Walt Rostow called for a troop increase of 8,000 to make "the United States a limited partner in the war." Soon other key administration figures like Secretary of State Dean Rusk and Secretary of Defense Robert McNamara joined the chorus of voices chanting loudly in favor of increasing American involvement.[13]

Secretary McNamara was especially influential in the Kennedy White House, and his views had a powerful impact on the decision to escalate. McNamara had no qualms about recommending a commitment of 200,000 American soldiers. Without any specific knowledge of the culture or history of the region, McNamara saw Vietnam in purely Western terms. As president of the Ford Motor Company McNamara had come to have great faith in quantifiable results, and he tended to ignore anything that could not be evaluated in purely statistical terms. Thus, when McNamara would talk about fighting the kind of war that would make the North bleed, he could not foresee that when the Viet Cong lost some 290,000 men in the 1960s, the North Vietnamese would simply send them 290,000 more. Robert McNamara was to learn eventually that the Viet Cong and North Vietnamese were more than willing to die for their cause. It was to be an expensive and costly lesson for the United States.[14]

Influenced by McNamara, Rusk, and the military thinkers like General Maxwell D. Taylor who argued that the Communists would not respond in a significant fashion to increasing American troop involvement, President Kennedy finally agreed to send "military advisers" to Vietnam. He was still smarting from the debacle of the Bay of Pigs, and his initial aim was for the Americans to avoid direct combat. As Kennedy said, the American mission in Vietnam was to "show [the South Vietnamese] how the job should be done—not to tell them or do it for them."[15]

But General Taylor was wrong. The Communists did respond, and American military personnel could hardly avoid being drawn slowly but inexorably into the vortex of what became the greatest tragedy in modern American history—the war in Vietnam. By 1962 there were 12,000 American troops in South Vietnam. Still, the Viet Cong, despite their brutality in the countryside, continued to gain ground. And by November 1963, the month in which John F. Kennedy was assassinated, 16,000 Americans were in Vietnam.[16]

The major problem Kennedy had with Vietnam was not with his enemies but with his friends. President Diem's regime was corrupt and extremely unpopular. Although the United States continued to pour equipment and supplies into Diem's Army of the Republic of Vietnam, it was like pouring money down a sinkhole.

Diem's ARVN army was ineffective. Instead of selecting his military leadership for their capabilities, Diem chose his top

Left to right: Secretary of Defense Robert S. McNamara, General Maxwell D. Taylor and President John F. Kennedy (John F. Kennedy Library)

generals and many officers for their loyalty, their Catholic religion and their political connections. On the other hand, the enlisted men in Diem's demoralized ARVN forces were often kidnapped from their impoverished villages and forced to serve. Obviously, their loyalty to Diem's stated goal of defeating the Communists was hardly overwhelming. Some probably even sided with the enemy.

Initially, the Americans, led by Ambassador Nolting, turned a blind eye to the corruption and weaknesses of the Diem regime. But as the trouble between the Diem regime and the Buddhists escalated, President Kennedy's roving ambassador, Averell Harriman, reported that Diem had to go, and that his regime could not last as long as it "continued to be repressive, dictatorial and unpopular." Harriman sharply denounced Ambassador Nolting, who had been supportive of the Diem regime.

Seeking bipartisan approval of his policies, on June 27, 1963 President Kennedy appointed Henry Cabot Lodge, Jr., his former Republican opponent in 1952, as his new envoy to South Vietnam. A few days later Kennedy summoned a number of close aides to the Oval Office to talk about Vietnam. For the first time, the Kennedy advisers discussed the distinct possibility of overthrowing the corrupt Diem regime by a coup d'etat (an illegal or forceful change of government).[17]

The role of Ambassador Henry Cabot Lodge was to see to it that Diem was overthrown but, at the same time, to distance the United States from complicity in the revolt. It was not an easy task, but the patrician Lodge, with presidential aspirations of his own, was up to the devious job ahead. At Lodge's request the Voice of America (a radio service promoting the U.S. point of view in foreign countries) was permitted to broadcast reports absolving the South Vietnamese army of any responsibility for attacking Buddhist temples. All of this had little to do with the Buddhists and much to do with the fact that the Kennedy administration was distancing itself from the Diem government.

Lodge, in daily contact with elements of the South Vietnamese army that were plotting to overthrow Diem, began to ask Washington for permission to give the rebel Vietnamese officers the green light. Lodge worried that any delay might strengthen President Diem's brother, Ngo Dinh Nhu, who was now reported to be flirting with the Communists. Nhu, concerned only with his own self-interest, cared little about politics. He just wanted to be on the winning side. When Lodge met with President Diem he suggested that Diem get rid of his corrupt brother. Lodge later recalled,

> I could see a cloud pass across his face when I suggested that he get rid of Nhu and improve his government. He absolutely refused to discuss any of the topics that President Kennedy had instructed me to raise, and that frankly jolted me.[18]

Ambassador Lodge, backed up by John Richardson, the CIA station chief in Saigon, was fully supportive of a rebellion led by high-ranking South Vietnamese officers. However, there were those in the administration like Vice President Johnson, Robert McNamara, Maxwell Taylor and CIA director John McCone who still opposed a coup against Diem, for two reasons. It was somewhat out of character, not to mention a betrayal, for the United States to be directly plotting the overthrow of a supposedly friendly (to the United States) government. More important, many in the Kennedy administration were not quite certain that the plotters were strong enough to actually overthrow Diem. Diem might not have been strong enough to suppress the Viet Cong, but no one knew for sure that he couldn't put down an American-orchestrated plot. And if by some chance the plotters were thwarted, the United States government could hardly escape the embarrassment of having given its go-ahead and support.

Still, Lodge continued to press the Kennedy administration. On August 29, 1963 he cabled Washington to demand some decisive instructions with which he could signal the plotters. Lodge wrote,

> We are launched on a course from which there is no respectable turning back: the overthrow of the Diem government. There is no turning back because U.S. prestige is already publicly committed to this end in large measure, and will become more so as the facts leak out. In a more fundamental sense, there is no turning back because there is no possibility, in my view, that the war can be won under a Diem administration.[19]

Lodge wanted American aid to Diem halted. That was the signal the South Vietnamese generals would need to spark their rebellion against Diem. President Kennedy, in an unprecedented move, gave Lodge complete authority to suspend American aid to Diem.[20]

That September, Kennedy himself took the initiative to explain his changing Southeast Asian policies to the American people. In a prime-time TV interview on September 2 with Walter Cronkite on CBS, President Kennedy publicly backed Lodge. In what seemed like a remarkable attack on a friendly government, Kennedy criticized Diem's Buddhist policies as "very unwise." Kennedy indicated that Diem's regime had lost "popular support." In effect, Kennedy had called for Diem's resignation.

Kennedy, upset that his Cronkite interview had been cut from 30 to 12 minutes that were mostly critical of Diem, agreed to an interview on NBC with David Brinkley and Chet Huntley—but only after the president was given final approval of what was broadcast. Kennedy was keenly aware that, with the nightly network news programs expanding from 15 to 30 minutes in September 1963, he could reach far more Americans in a few minutes than he could by talking to dozens of newspaper reporters for hours. And he wanted his Vietnam policies stated clearly to the public.[21]

President Diem's last chance came in late September, when President Kennedy sent Robert McNamara and General Maxwell Taylor to Vietnam. They carried a letter, written by Kennedy, putting Diem on notice that the United States was running out of patience and that if Diem continued his policies, especially his refusal to remove his brother Nhu, President Kennedy was prepared to withdraw all American troops and support from Vietnam.

In part Kennedy wrote Diem, "we do not wish to cut off our aid programs at this time, but it would be wrong for me not to let you know that a change is inevitable unless the situation in Vietnam takes a major visible and credible turn for the better."

Instead of delivering the president's letter to Diem, McNamara and Taylor chose to convey Kennedy's message themselves in order to give the South Vietnamese leader some room to maneuver. But Diem wouldn't budge and instead lectured the Americans, asserting that his problems were mainly due to an inflammatory American press.[22]

The end came for Diem on November 1 when some Vietnamese army units led by General Duong Van Minh (Big Minh) surrounded Diem's Saigon palace while capturing the police headquarters and the radio station. At first Diem and his brother reacted calmly, certain that with American support their troops would remain loyal. President Diem, unaware that the CIA and the State Department had been in collusion with his rebel generals, telephoned Lodge, saying, "Some units have made a rebellion, and I want to know what is the attitude of the United States." Lodge's answer was careful and circumspect. He responded, "I do not feel well enough informed to be able to tell you. I have heard the shooting, but am not acquainted with all the facts. Also, it is four-thirty A.M. in Washington, and the U.S. government cannot possibly have a view."[23]

Soon it became apparent to Diem that his government could not survive. On November 2, Diem, hiding in a French church in Cholon, surrendered. Complicated negotiations for the escape of Diem and Nhu from Vietnam broke down because the Kennedy administration, worried about being embarrassed by their presence in the United States, refused to offer them asylum. Both men, now captured by the generals who had despised them for many years, were murdered on the road to Saigon. President Kennedy was told of Diem's assassination while meeting with Maxwell Taylor and other aides. The president, according to Taylor, "rushed from the room with a look of shock and dismay on his face."[24]

Clearly, Kennedy realized that he had put a series of events into motion that had gotten far out of hand. While the Vietnamese generals issued a statement in Saigon saying that the deaths of Diem and Nhu were suicides, President Kennedy knew the truth. Four days after Diem's murder, in a cable to President Kennedy, Ambassador Lodge gave Kennedy an accurate assessment of what had taken place. Lodge wrote that the rebellion had been a Vietnamese action that "we could neither manage nor stop after it got started." However, demonstrating that the United States was clearly a powerful influence in the movement of the historical forces that led to Diem's overthrow, Lodge added, "It is equally certain that the ground in which the coup seed grew into a robust plant was prepared by us, and that the coup would not have happened [as] it did without our preparation."[25]

Within three weeks of the overthrow of Diem, President Kennedy himself would be dead. The coup in Vietnam was followed by 18 months of unstable leadership in which one Vietnamese general after another stepped up and was in turn overthrown. The North Vietnamese, encouraged by the instability in the South, grew bolder and increased their support of the Viet Cong. As a result, Presidents Lyndon B. Johnson and Richard M. Nixon would eventually send more than 550,000 American servicemen to Vietnam to test their cold war faith in falling dominoes. Some 53,000 young Americans would die for a questionable policy that tore apart the fabric of American society in the 1960s—a policy continued under Kennedy's watch.

Just what would President Kennedy have done had he lived? Would the youthful president, a cold warrior who so admired American toughness, courage and bravado, have had the wisdom to take U.S. troops out of a war they could not win and out of a country few Americans understood? One historian, William J. Rust, writes, "My guess is that he [Kennedy] would not have crossed the covert action-advisory threshold, would not have bombed North Vietnam, and would not have committed U.S. ground troops to South Vietnam. Undoubtedly, Kennedy would have put off the really hard choices in Vietnam until after the 1964 election."[26]

Another scholar, John M. Newman, asks, "would Kennedy have sent in the combat troops as Johnson did? The answer to that is no." It was Kennedy's undelivered speech at the Dallas Trade Mart that Kennedy critics have used to argue that, like Lyndon Johnson, Kennedy too would have raised U.S. combat strength in Vietnam. Newman, however, disagrees. He cites National Security Action Memorandum-111, issued on November 22, 1961, as proof that "Kennedy would never have placed American combat troops in Vietnam."

Newman writes, "Kennedy concluded that a retreat from Vietnam could not happen until after he was reelected." Newman believes that had he lived Kennedy might have taken the truth about Vietnam to the American people in 1964—that the war was essentially unwinnable.[27]

Other historians argue that Kennedy would have escalated the war. David Burner writes, "It is ironic that most Americans remember that their country somehow went downhill after Kennedy's death, yet the down escalator was the Vietnam War in which he played a principal role. Withdrawing from Vietnam would have taken the kind of political courage this pragmatic president so much admired yet so rarely demonstrated."[28]

But perhaps Kennedy was looking for a way out of Vietnam. On November 21, before Kennedy left for Texas, he told his aide Mike Forrestal, "When you get back, after the first of the year, I want you to organize an in-depth study of every possible option we've got in Vietnam, including how to get out of there. We have to review this whole thing from the bottom to the top."[29]

The next day the president was assassinated in Dallas, Texas.

Notes

1. Quoted in Richard Reeves, *President Kennedy: Profile of Power* (New York, 1993), p. 31; See also Hugh Sidey, *John F. Kennedy, President* (New York, 1964), p. 32.
2. William J. Rust, *Kennedy in Vietnam: American Vietnam Policy 1960–1963* (New York, 1985), pp. xiii–xv.
3. David Burner, *John F. Kennedy and a New Generation* (Boston, 1988), p. 95.
4. Ibid., p. 96.
5. Walter LaFeber, *America, Russia, and the Cold War 1945–1984* (New York, 1985), p. 232.
6. John M. Newman, *JFK and Vietnam: Deception, Intrigue and the Struggle for Power* (New York, 1992), p. 3; and quoted in Reeves, *President Kennedy,* p. 46. Actually, Eisenhower *had* mentioned Vietnam. JFK was not generally known to be a good listener.
7. Burner, *John F. Kennedy and a New Generation,* pp. 97–98.
8. David Halberstam, *The Best and the Brightest* (New York, 1972), p. 129.
9. William L. O'Neill, *Coming Apart: An Informal History of America in the 1960's* (Chicago, 1971), p. 78.

10. Newman, *JFK and Vietnam,* pp. 331–332.
11. Ibid., pp. 333–334.
12. Burner, *John F. Kennedy and a New Generation,* p. 96.
13. Ibid., pp. 98–99.
14. Ibid., p. 99.
15. Ibid., pp. 100–101.
16. LaFeber, *America, Russia, and the Cold War,* p. 233. See also Burner, *John F. Kennedy and a New Generation,* p. 101.
17. Stanley Karnow, *Vietnam: A History* (New York, 1983), p. 282.
18. Ibid., pp. 288–289.
19. Ibid.
20. Ibid., p. 290.
21. Montague Kern, Patricia W. Levering, and Ralph B. Levering, *The Kennedy Crises: The Press, the Presidency, and Foreign Policy* (Chapel Hill, North Carolina, 1983), pp. 165–166.
22. Reeves, *President Kennedy,* p. 609.
23. Karnow, *Vietnam,* p. 307.
24. Ibid., pp. 310–311.
25. Ibid., p. 295.
26. Rust, *Kennedy in Vietnam,* p. 181.
27. Newman, *JFK and Vietnam,* pp. 457–459.
28. Burner, *John F. Kennedy and a New Generation,* p. 113.
29. Reeves, *President Kennedy,* p. 660.

10

ASSASSINATION IN DALLAS

"My God, I'm hit!"

On November 22, 1963, at approximately 12:30 P.M., an open blue Lincoln convertible limousine that carried President Kennedy and his wife, Jacqueline, in the back seat and Texas governor John Connally and his wife, Nellie, in the jump seats, with two Secret Service agents, Roy Kellerman and Bill Greer, in the front seat, made a fateful turn onto Dealey Plaza in Dallas. The president had come to Texas to mend some Democratic political fences in a vital state he needed to win if he wanted to keep the White House in 1964.

As the president's limo turned past a seven-story red-brick building, then called the Texas School Book Depository, it made a hard left heading toward a railway underpass 200 yards away. As the car moved slowly toward the tunnel Jackie Kennedy could recall thinking in the noon heat, "How pleasant the cool tunnel will be."

Abraham Zapruder, a New York dress manufacturer who had moved to Dallas, crouching on a low concrete abutment between the Book Depository and the underpass, had just snapped the telephoto lens of his 8 mm home movie camera and was filming the president's limo as it approached. The film was in color.[1]

Just as the Kennedy car entered Zapruder's viewfinder, the sound of rifle fire marred the warm welcome the Kennedys and their party seemed to be receiving from the large crowds of Dallas citizens who had lined up along the route of the presidential motorcade.

Everyone seemed to hear different sounds as the Lincoln moved slowly towards that tunnel at 11.2 miles an hour. Jackie Kennedy thought she heard a motorcycle noise. Some people in other cars of the president's motorcade thought it was a backfire from a car or truck. But most of the experienced hunters knew immediately that what they had heard was the chilling sound of rifle fire.[2]

The initial shot, a 6.5 millimeter bullet, struck President Kennedy (either from the front or the back—the evidence is so uncertain that scholars and forensic specialists have not reached complete agreement on this point)[3] in the throat, nicking the knot of his blue patterned tie and causing Kennedy to slump slightly forward as he brought his hands up to his throat as if he were choking himself. But Kennedy wasn't grimacing. He appeared, if anything, genuinely surprised.

Secret Service Agent Roy Kellerman thought he heard President Kennedy shout in his unmistakable voice, "My God, I'm hit!" Kellerman looked over his left shoulder and Agent Bill Greer looked over his right shoulder. They both could see that the president of the United States had indeed been hit.

Governor Connally was hit next as a bullet (or the same bullet that hit Kennedy—later called "the magic bullet" because of its near-perfect condition after doing so much damage) smashed into his back, through his chest and wrist, halting its erratic path to embed itself in his thigh. Connally, seeing his legs covered with blood, shouted, "No, no, no, no, no! They're going to kill us both."

Jackie Kennedy heard him, and in that brief terrible instant of tragedy, before her brain had fully programmed what her eyes could see and her ears could hear, the First Lady wondered why Connally was screaming as she began to turn anxiously toward her husband.

Another bullet went wide of the target(s) and hit the roadway, fragmenting and nicking the cheek of a bystander. As the Secret Service men tried to react instantly to protect the First Family as they had been trained to do, the loud report from the rifle startled a flock of pigeons, who quickly swarmed into the bright azure Dallas sky overhead.[4]

The president's limousine was still moving slowly and had barely gone a few yards from the base of a grassy knoll that was topped along its rear by a six-foot white picket fence. At that instant a final shot hit President Kennedy, exploding the right side of his head and hurling him violently to the left and then backward. The First Lady leaned toward her mortally wounded husband, still uncertain about what had happened. The president appeared to have a puzzled look on his face. Jackie Kennedy then watched in horror as "in a gesture of infinite grace, he raised his right hand, as though to brush back his tousled chestnut hair. But the motion faltered. The hand fell back limply. He had been reaching for the top of his head. But it wasn't there any more."[5]

Jacqueline Kennedy reacted instinctively. With the blood and brain matter of her husband sprayed all over her pink suit, she sprang up on her knees shouting out, "My God, what are they doing? My God, they've killed Jack, they've killed my husband." She then tried to climb across the sloping rear of the car and was only saved from serious injury by the intervention of Secret Service Agent Clint Hill, who forced her back into the limo. Later, Mrs. Kennedy could not remember climbing onto the back of the car.

Meanwhile, Agent Kellerman barked at the driver Greer, "Let's get out of here; we are hit." Then Kellerman radioed ahead to the lead car: "Lawson, this is Kellerman. Get us to the hospital immediately."[6]

As the limo picked up speed, heading for Parkland Memorial Hospital four miles away, Mrs. Kennedy cradled the mortally wounded president in her lap crying, "Oh, my God, they have shot my husband. I love you Jack."[7]

Within minutes of the shooting, Dallas police and Secret Service agents fanned out all over the area as confusion and general pandemonium seemed to reign supreme. One police officer, rushing into the Book Depository building, came upon a newly hired stockboy drinking a Coke in the second floor lunchroom within moments of the shooting. The cop pulled his gun, but when someone told him that the young man, Lee Harvey Oswald, was an employee, the officer hurried off to the sixth floor, where witnesses had reported seeing a rifleman at one of the windows.[8]

On the sixth floor, concealed behind some cardboard boxes of textbooks, the authorities found a World War II Italian-made Mannlicher-Carcano rifle with the serial number C2766. Whoever had fired it had vanished.[9]

Arriving at Parkland Hospital, the president was immediately rushed into a trauma room, where a team of doctors worked frantically on him. Mrs. Kennedy refused to leave the room, choosing to remain by her husband's side. At one point Dr. Kemp Clark turned to the First Lady, saying, "Your husband has sustained a fatal wound." "I know," Jacqueline Kennedy softly replied.

Dr. George Burkley reached over to check President Kennedy's pulse and could feel nothing. At approximately 1 P.M., a half-hour after the shooting, swallowing hard, Dr. Burkley said, "The president is dead." Kennedy was then given the last rites of the Catholic Church by Father Oscar L. Huber, a local priest.

At 1:15 P.M., 15 minutes after President Kennedy was pronounced dead, J. D. Tippitt, a Dallas police officer, was shot to death on a sidewalk several miles from the scene of the assassination in Dealey Plaza. Police were informed by a caller that a man had rushed into the Texas Theater, eight blocks from the Tippitt shooting, without paying for a ticket. Police and FBI agents immediately converged on the theater (it has never been made entirely clear why so many law enforcement personnel were so concerned about a man who had snuck into a sparsely crowded movie theater on the afternoon of the murder of a president).

After a brief scuffle during which the man, the same Lee Harvey Oswald who had been briefly stopped at the Book Depository, tried to shoot a Dallas police officer (Oswald's gun misfired), the police and federal agents subdued him. Oswald cried out, "Well, it's all over now!" He then shouted, "I protest this police brutality," as the lawmen hustled him out of the theater, past an angry crowd and into a waiting car, where Oswald was rushed to police headquarters in downtown Dallas.[10]

Starting with interrogation sessions led by Captain Will Fritz on the third floor of the Police and Courts building in the homicide and robbery bureau, for the next 23 hours Oswald never wavered in his claim that he had nothing to do with shooting the president of the United States. "I'm just a patsy," he told reporters when permitted a brief passing moment with the press. "I didn't shoot anybody, no sir." Later, Oswald would say, "Nobody has told me anything except that I am accused of, of, [sic] murdering a policeman. I know nothing more than that and I do request that someone come forward to give me legal assistance." When asked by a reporter directly, "Did you kill the President?" Oswald responded,

> No. I have not been charged with that. In fact nobody has said that to me yet. The first thing I heard about it was when the newspaper reporters in the hall asked me that question.[11]

There was never a chance for the state to prove whether Oswald's claims were true or false. Two days after the Kennedy assassination, as Oswald was being transferred to the county jail, he was shot to death before a national television audience by Jack Ruby, a local night club operator. Ruby had a close relationship with a number of Dallas police officers and had somehow been permitted to enter the basement of the police building with a .38 caliber revolver concealed in his jacket pocket.[12]

The new president, Lyndon B. Johnson, quickly convened a federal commission headed by Supreme Court Chief Justice Earl Warren. The Warren Commission also included Congressman Gerald R. Ford and former CIA head Allen W. Dulles, who had been fired by President Kennedy. Few Americans were surprised in 1964 when the Warren Commission issued its 26-volume report, essentially concluding that Lee Harvey Oswald, acting alone, had killed the president as well as Dallas patrolman Tippitt. Oswald, a former marine who had defected to Russia, married a Russian woman, and returned to the United States, had owned the rifle used to kill the president, had brought the rifle to the Texas School Book Depository on the morning of the assassination, and thus "was the assassin of President Kennedy."[13]

The Warren Commission also found no evidence that either Oswald or Jack Ruby "was part of any conspiracy, domestic or foreign, to assassinate President Kennedy."[14]

The Warren Commission was immediately attacked by a number of writers, scholars and assassination buffs. While it is beyond the scope of this study to go into those attacks, over 2,000 books have been written on the assassination of President John F. Kennedy. Among those accused of killing Kennedy are the Mafia, the CIA, the FBI, the Cubans, the Russians and even Lyndon B. Johnson.[15]

In February 1967 the district attorney of New Orleans, Jim Garrison, announced that he had solved the mystery. A little later Garrison arrested Clay Shaw, a prominent local businessman, whom Garrison charged with conspiring with Oswald to assassinate President Kennedy. In a widely publicized conspiracy trial, Shaw was acquitted in 1969 as Garrison tried to make a case that Kennedy was killed because he was about to withdraw the United States from Vietnam. But Garrison could provide no evidence other than what was already known, and a jury quickly found Shaw not guilty.

However, by that time the American public was convinced that the Warren Commission was tainted. A Harris poll indicated that 60% of the American public believed that Kennedy was killed by conspirators. The problem was that everybody had a different theory of just who the conspirators were, and the Kennedy family did not help very much, instead doing all they could to block legitimate scholars and researchers from looking at the vital medical evidence—probably for reasons of good taste. But nevertheless, the crucial autopsy reports and photographs have been locked up tightly in the National Archives until sometime in the middle of the 21st century.

The conspiracy theorists were bolstered 10 years later when the House Select Committee on Assassinations concluded that there was a "95 percent probability" that President Kennedy had been the victim of a conspiracy—just as District Attorney Garrison had charged.

The debate was revived by Hollywood director Oliver Stone in 1991 when his much-publicized film *JFK* pointed to a broad-based conspiracy in Kennedy's assassination. Stone's film, starring Kevin Costner as District Attorney Jim Garrison, was hotly debated by scholars and film critics. But in the end, little about the death of President Kennedy was really resolved by Stone's cinematic flights of historical fancy.

A recent book, *Case Closed: Lee Harvey Oswald and the Assassination of JFK* by Gerald Posner, returns to the earliest theory of the disputed Warren Commission report: that "Lee Harvey Oswald, driven by his own twisted and impenetrable furies, was the only assassin at Dealey Plaza on November 22, 1963."[16]

Thus, one thing about the assassination of John F. Kennedy remains clear: in all likelihood we will never know with any certainty why John F. Kennedy was killed and whether Lee Harvey Oswald, who was obviously involved, acted alone. In this sense, history and the American people have been scandalously cheated by the unsolved mystery surrounding the murder of the president. As one historian accurately noted in 1971, "Like UFO's, it seemed the assassination of John F. Kennedy would always puzzle us."[17]

Notes

1. William Manchester, *The Death of a President, November, 1963* (New York, 1967), p. 131, p. 152, p. 170, and p. 175.
2. Ibid., p. 177.
3. Ibid., p. 178.
4. Ibid., p. 180.
5. Ibid., p. 180.
6. Quoted in Ibid., pp. 182–183; also quoted in *Report of the Warren Commission on the Assassination of President Kennedy* (New York, 1964), p. 63.
7. *Report of the Warren Commission,* p. 62.
8. Ibid., pp. 141–142.
9. Ibid., p. 122.
10. Manchester, *The Death of a President,* p. 215 and pp. 320–323.
11. *Report of the Warren Commission,* pp. 184–189; and Robert Sam Anson, "The Shooting of JFK," *Esquire,* November 1991, p. 95.
12. *Report of the Warren Commission,* p. 201.
13. Ibid., p. 183.
14. Ibid., p. 41.
15. For further investigation see Anthony Summers, *Conspiracy* (New York, 1989); Henry Hurt, Reasonable Doubt: An Investigation into the Assassination of John F. Kennedy (New York, 1985); David S. Lifton, Best Evidence: Disguise and Deception in the Assassination of John F. Kennedy (New York, 1980); and Edward J. Epstein, *Inquest* (New York, 1966), *Counterplot* (New York, 1969), and *Legend: The Secret World of Lee Harvey Oswald* (New

York, 1978). All three of Epstein's books have recently been republished in one volume, *The Assassination Chronicles* (New York, 1992).

16. Gerald Posner, *Case Closed: Lee Harvey Oswald and the Assassination of JFK* (New York, 1993), p. 472.

17. William L. O'Neill, *Coming Apart: An Informal History of America in the 1960's* (Chicago, 1971), p. 103.

11

JOHN F. KENNEDY AT THE GATES OF HISTORY

"Ask every person if he's heard the story
And tell it strong and clear if he has not
That once there was a fleeting wisp of glory
called Camelot . . .
Don't let it be forgot
That once there was a spot
For one brief shining moment
That was known as Camelot."

King Arthur from the Broadway
musical Camelot

"It all ended, as it began, in the cold."
Arthur M. Schlesinger, Jr.

When John F. Kennedy was assassinated on November 22, 1963 the nation seemed to come to a screeching halt as if frozen in time. Many historians still date the most tumultuous decade in 20th-century American history from the day John F. Kennedy was shot.

The immediate image that most Americans of the baby boomer generation would retain, promoted by the president's widow and his politically ambitious family, would be of the brave young king leading his fellow knights of the Washington Round Table. The myth that John F. Kennedy, struck down in the prime of his reign, presided over a modern-day Camelot is still being encouraged to this day by the Kennedy family and the Democratic Party.

Every four years the Democratic National Convention becomes a showcase for aspiring politicians to revive the Kennedy

Jacqueline Kennedy Onassis, who died in 1994, helped to preserve the image of her husband as a young king struck down in his prime. Here she is pictured with Kitty Dukakis. (Boston Ledger)

myth and legend. Nearly every Democratic politician, and not a few Republicans, strive for the day when the media, hungry to recreate what has been misperceived as a glorious era, compares them to the youth and vigor that had been projected by the slain hero of Camelot.

On the day before he was inaugurated, January 19, 1993, President-elect Bill Clinton made a pilgrimage to pay homage at the Kennedy graveside by the eternal flame in Arlington, Virginia.

Hardly a press briefing passes in which President Clinton, who met President Kennedy as a teenager on the White House lawn, fails to make reference to the man he credits with influencing his decision to pursue a career in politics. In May 1993 alone, President Clinton made four public references to the Kennedy presidency. And on October 29, 1993 Clinton appeared with the entire Kennedy clan, including the late president's widow and two children, to extol the Kennedy presidency and open the newly refurbished Kennedy Library in Boston. The *Boston Globe* reported,

When President Clinton arrives in Boston tonight to dedicate the JFK Library's new museum, it will be his fifth major event of the year with a Kennedyesque theme. Unlike former Presidents Jimmy Carter and Lyndon Johnson, Clinton does not bristle at comparisons with the Kennedys. He seems to welcome them.[1]

How did John F. Kennedy pass so quickly from a flesh-and-blood human being into the stuff of political myth and Round Table legend? Were the Kennedy years as filled with accomplishment as the Kennedyites claim or as bad as the recent critics now charge?

It began almost immediately after the assassination. America was hypnotized by the stark image of two beautiful, newly fatherless children standing obediently by their grieving, widowed mother as the funeral cortege made its painfully silent passage through the streets of Washington. There was the touching soldier-boy salute by little John-John—offered without guile, but not without direction—to his martyred father and to the riderless horse that followed the flag-draped presidential casket. Images. Images that were designed to tug at the frayed heartstrings of a shocked and grieving nation.

President John F. Kennedy (John F. Kennedy Library)

Thus, in its death, the Kennedy presidency, which had been so largely based on imagery, enshrined itself in an endless series of images on the television screens of a grief-stricken nation. Twenty years later, writer Henry Fairlie would pose an interesting question:

> Did John F. Kennedy exist? The question is not facile. It is the natural response of anyone who followed the nation's month-long observance of the twentieth anniversary of his assassination. From the scores of network and local television programs, from the millions of words that appeared in newspapers and magazines, from the books pasted together for the occasion, we ought to have been able to learn more of the man and the politician, of the achievements of his Administration, and perhaps above all, more of the meaning of the legend of Camelot to the American people now. And what we did learn was that Kennedy has not been placed in the American mind: that the legend of Camelot has faded, and the reality of those years has not yet been grasped.[2]

Within months of his death the Kennedy image makers began to break into print to help shape the Kennedy legend. Tom Wicker, a columnist for the *New York Times,* couldn't help but wax nostalgic about the Kennedy promise—a promise that would remain forever unfulfilled—in an *Esquire* article he wrote called "Kennedy Without Tears." Noting the incomparable Kennedy wit and style, Wicker wrote, "Six months after his death, John F. Kennedy is certain to take his place in American lore as one of those sure-sell heroes out of whose face or words or monuments a souvenir dealer can turn a steady buck."[3]

Wicker, however, hoped that future historians would examine John F. Kennedy as the very real political man that he was. Pointing to Kennedy's generally lackluster years in the Senate, Wicker continued,

> I thought Richard Nixon was perhaps a more interesting man than Kennedy. . . . But Kennedy, I thought then, for all his charm and fire and eloquence, was a straightforward political man, who listened to his own rhetoric, contrived his "image" in the comforting faith that a statesman had to get elected before he could do anyone any good,

and believed sincerely that his causes were not only right but actually offered solutions to human problems.[4]

The first in a series of pro-Kennedy books, painting the fallen president in a heroic and positive light, were written by those who served in his administration. In 1965 Kennedy aides Arthur M. Schlesinger, Jr.'s *A Thousand Days: John F. Kennedy in the White House,* and Theodore Sorensen's *Kennedy* became instant best-sellers. These books celebrated Kennedy's achievements and enshrined the Camelot legend. Still, they are indispensable tools to a full, if somewhat incomplete, understanding of the events that shaped Kennedy the man and Kennedy the president. Schlesinger especially viewed Kennedy in heroic terms, concluding, "He re-established the republic as the first generation of our leaders saw it—young, brave, civilized, rational, gay, tough, questing, exultant in the excitement and potentiality of history. He transformed the American spirit."[5] And Sorensen, already aware of the growing legend, wrote,

> history will remember John Kennedy for what he started as well as for what he completed. The forces he released in this world will be felt for generations to come. The standards he set, the goals he outlined and the talented men he attracted to politics and public service will influence this country's course for at least a decade. . . . People will remember not only what he did but what he stood for. . . . In my view, the man was greater than the legend. His life, not his death, created his greatness.[6]

Within a few years virtually every Kennedy friend, political associate and family retainee chimed in with "life and times" books that, while hagiographic (writing about Kennedy as if he were a saint), are still valuable for some insight into his life and times, character and personality.

The first of several highly critical studies of the Kennedy presidency was the 1973 book *The Kennedy Promise* by Henry Fairlie. Fairlie, totally unimpressed with Kennedy's abilities as a leader, argued that "John Kennedy's achievements were less significant than those of (11th President) James K. Polk." Fairlie charged that Kennedy and his brothers rose to power by literally outspending their political rivals over the years. "In an important sense," Fairlie says, "the family bought its political influence."[7]

, In Fairlie's view, the Kennedy White House was ineffective because John F. Kennedy wanted it that way. Kennedy, in Fairlie's eyes, was the kind of president who only heard what he wanted to hear and would hardly brook dissent among his tight inner circle of advisers. In Fairlie's opinion only yes-men worked for JFK. He said,

> Whether in the advice which he sought while he was a candidate, or in the task forces which he asked to report to him while he was the President-elect, or in the ad hoc task forces which he employed while he was the President, John Kennedy usually contrived to receive the kind of advice which he wished.[8]

Fairlie faults the Kennedy administration on civil rights, on domestic as well as foreign policy, and on manipulating the press. In almost every crucial policy area, Fairlie charges the Kennedy administration with failure. Under Kennedy, Fairlie says, politics had become theater. He writes, "The guerilla was theatre; the fifty-mile hike was theatre; the crisis councils were theatre; and the American people imagined that they were real."[9]

Fairlie's harsh verdict on Kennedy was not to be taken lightly. Fairlie's work was quite different from earlier hatchet jobs on Kennedy. Henry Fairlie, an English journalist, was widely known and well respected. Other scholars took Fairlie seriously when he theorized,

> John Kennedy proclaimed in measures and in messages that he wished to do so much; but he in fact achieved so little that the people could hardly be blamed if they concluded that their political processes were inadequate to their tasks. If a leader of such exceptional vigour, commanding an administration of such unusual talents, could not achieve his purposes, there must be something at fault with the political institutions which balked him. The fact that he was not, from day to day, exercising any political leadership within these institutions went unnoticed.[10]

Other critical studies of John F. Kennedy soon followed. In 1975, Lewis J. Paper published *John F. Kennedy: The Promise and the Performance.* Paper criticized every aspect of the Kennedy presidency, noting that style often took the place of substance in the administration. Challenging Kennedy's method of White House decision making, Paper wrote, "There was . . . a natural reaction among many to inflate the meaning of Kennedy's fluent rhetoric and to attach unfounded significance to those words after his death; the accomplishments of his New Frontier were often measured by phrases instead of by concrete results."[11]

In 1976 Joan and Clay Blair, Jr. published *The Search for J.F.K.*, focusing on Kennedy's early life and especially on the crucial years between 1935 and 1947. The Blairs based their research on an extensive examination of materials from the new Kennedy Library and were the first scholars to show how the family had covered up Kennedy's serious health problems up through 1947, when Kennedy was diagnosed with Addison's disease. Their work corrected the myths surrounding Kennedy's abilities as a student and a literary talent.

A 1992 study that was heavily criticized by the Kennedy family, *JFK: Reckless Youth* by Nigel Hamilton, sheds much-needed light on Kennedy's early life and, although it hardly fits the Kennedy myth and image, seems for the most part based on accurate and reliable sources. Kennedy emerges as a rich and spoiled youngster whose parents were somewhat neglectful of their many children—a dysfunctional family.

The most critical analysis of John F. Kennedy was one published in 1991 by Thomas C. Reeves, entitled *A Question of Character: A Life of John F. Kennedy*. Reeves, a University of Wisconsin history professor, assails Kennedy's character, writing that "the image of the man has . . . overwhelmed the reality of his life." Reeves says that Kennedy was a man of low moral fiber, noting,

> During the Thousand Days, Kennedy arrogantly and irresponsibly violated his covenant with the people. While saying and doing the appropriate things in the public light, he acted covertly in ways that seriously demeaned himself and his office. He got away with it at the time, and the cover-up that followed kept the truth hidden for decades.[12]

However, Kennedy is not without his champions in the scholarly community. There are those studies that, while admitting Kennedy's shortcomings, see his unfinished presidency and his leadership in a more positive light. In his 1991 book *Promises Kept: John F. Kennedy's New Frontier,* Irving Bernstein argued persuasively that Kennedy was just emerging as a leader of great stature when he was cut down. As proof Bernstein cites the fact that Kennedy's entire program was enacted within 18 months of his death.

One of the best studies of the Kennedy years was *President Kennedy: Profile of Power* by Richard Reeves, published in 1993. Reeves attempts to take the reader into the inner sanctum of the Kennedy presidency, and it almost seems as if one is eavesdropping on private presidential conversations. Reeves tells his reader that his narrative is about what John F. Kennedy actually did during his three years in the White House. Reeves notes, "What I searched for was what he knew or heard, said or read." He says,

> The man at the center was a gifted professional politician reacting to events he often neither foresaw nor understood, handling some well, others badly, but always ready with plausible explanations. He was intelligent, detached, curious, candid if not always honest, and he was careless and dangerously disorganized. He was also very impatient, addicted to excitement, living his life as if it were a race against boredom.[13]

Richard Reeves goes far beyond the simplistic moralizing of so many other Kennedy critics. He writes, "the most important thing about Kennedy was not a great political decision, though he made some, but his own political ambition. He did not wait his turn. . . . He believed (and proved) that the only qualification for the most powerful job in the world was wanting it."[14]

Reeves, however, is not unsympathetic to Kennedy. He notes, "John F. Kennedy was one of only forty-two men who truly know what it is like to be President. He was not prepared for it, but I doubt that anyone ever was or will be. The job is sui generis [unique]. The presidency is an act of faith."[15]

Where does all this leave us? Clearly, the imagery of John F. Kennedy, from his powerful inaugural address delivered with such sparkling clarity and promise in 1961 to his 1963 *"Ich bin ein Berliner*" (I am a Berliner) speech at the Berlin Wall to the intense period of national mourning after his death conveys the notion that the Kennedy presidency was a time of great activity and a period of heroic national progress.

In the brief three years that he led the nation, great and important changes were taking place. The infant civil rights movement, put into motion during the more placid 1950s, was exploding on the American scene with a force that John F. Kennedy could neither understand nor stop. It was a freight train going downhill, and Kennedy's only option was either to get on board or to get out of the way. Although he hopped that train a little late, he still became a full-fledged passenger who could see the ultimate virtue in the destination.

In the area of foreign policy, where he was supposed to have entered the White House with some degree of expertise, the Kennedy report card is at least a passing grade—a C at best. His abject failure at the Bay of Pigs was balanced out by his victory over Khrushchev during the missile crisis of October 1962. Still, in a dangerous game of nuclear Russian roulette, the fact that Kennedy and the American people emerged as winners is comforting only in retrospect. One shudders to think what the results might have been had Kennedy's risky gamble not succeeded.

On Vietnam, President Kennedy must be given a failing grade. It was, after all, on his watch that over 16,000 American GIs were sent to Southeast Asia. And hypothesizing on what Kennedy would have done is not at all relevant. In the end, he listened to poor advice and did what he did. The nation, for over a dozen years, paid a heavy price for Kennedy's poor judgment and military bravado.

Still, there is an immeasurable quality to the Kennedy presidency. As president, John F. Kennedy served in a real and symbolic way to energize an entire generation of young Americans who believed in the possibility of progress and positive change. It was the last time Americans felt really good about themselves as Americans. Much of this was due to Kennedy.

The powerful zest for public service is testified to by the Peace Corps, a major Kennedy initiative; and the integrated nature of the civil rights movement, with many whites caring as much about the quest for equality as blacks, is a testament to the leadership and examples set by John and Robert Kennedy.

Those examples, symbolic or otherwise, should not be diminished.

On the other hand, it would be just as great a mistake to make a hero out of Kennedy, as the myth-makers have done. As Ralph G. Martin says in *A Hero For Our Time,* John F. Kennedy was

> Not a myth. He was a very real human being full of his own foibles, his own doubts, his own weaknesses. Not a great president. There was the growth of the man in office, the pragmatism that turned into passion on big issues, the courage that became wisdom. But there was no time to prove his potential. Still, he was a hero for our time. In some mysterious way, he did inspire in so many millions of people all over the world a great excitement of hope. That excitement was real. . . . That excitement still lingers.[16]

Students of the Kennedy years would be wise to pay close attention to the words of historian Eugene D. Genovese, who has cogently observed that "those who look to history to provide glorious moments and heroes invariably are betrayed into making catastrophic errors in political judgment."[17]

Instead, John F. Kennedy should be seen as a flesh-and-blood human being and understood in the context of the perilous times in which he lived. Alex Beam, a *Boston Globe* columnist, recently noted that

> the Kennedy charisma is very real, and writing from inside the striped tents at Hyannis or Hickory Hill is more pleasant—and generally more productive—than working from the outside. Although it hardly excuses our subjective reporting, millions of Massachusetts residents love the Kennedys. . . . the public craves the myth, not the man.[18]

Or, as Arthur M. Schlesinger, Jr. lamented in 1983,

> He glittered when he lived, and the whole world grieved when he died. In the twenty years since, his memory has undergone vicissitude. Grief nourishes myth. The slain hero, robbed of fulfillment by tragic fate, is the stuff of legend. But legend has a short run in modern times. "Every hero," as Emerson said, "becomes a bore at last." So in

retrospect John F. Kennedy, the slain hero, the bonny prince, the king at the Round Table, the incarnation of youth and glamour and magic, is the object of disillusionment and the target of attack.

The whole idea of Camelot excites derision. In fact I am sure Kennedy would have derided it himself.[19]

Finally, if it is difficult to rate John F. Kennedy on a presidential spectrum with any accuracy, it is not hard to relate his significance to the nation at large in 1963. When Kennedy was killed, Washington columnist Mary McGrory told Daniel Patrick Moynihan (now a United States senator from New York), "We will never laugh again." "Oh, Mary, we'll laugh again," Moynihan sadly replied. "But we'll never be young again."

Notes

1. "Bill Clinton's Daily J.F.K. Calendar," *Time*, May 31, 1993, p. 16. See also *Boston Globe*, October 29, 1993, p. 3.
2. Henry Fairlie, "J.F.K.'s Television Presidency," *The New Republic*, December 26, 1983, p. 11.
3. Tom Wicker, "Kennedy Without Tears," *Smiling Through the Apocalypse: Esquire's History of the Sixties* (New York, 1987), p. 31.
4. Ibid., p. 33.
5. Arthur M. Schlesinger, Jr., *A Thousand Days: John F. Kennedy in the White House* (Boston, 1965), p. 1031.
6. Theodore C. Sorensen, *Kennedy* (New York, 1965), pp. 757–758.
7. Henry Fairlie, *The Kennedy Promise: The Politics of Expectation* (Garden City, New York, 1973), p. 1 and p. 43.
8. Ibid., p. 152.
9. Ibid., pp. 207–208.
10. Ibid., p. 344.
11. Lewis J. Paper, *John F. Kennedy: The Promise and the Performance* (New York, 1979), p. 211.
12. Thomas C. Reeves, *A Question of Character: A Life of John F. Kennedy* (New York, 1991), p. 17 and p. 421.
13. Richard Reeves, *President Kennedy: Profile of Power* (New York, 1993), pp. 18–19.
14. Ibid., p. 14.

15. Ibid., p. 20.
16. Ralph G. Martin, *A Hero for Our Time: An Intimate Story of the Kennedy Years* (New York, 1983), p. 508.
17. Eugene D. Genovese, *In Red and Black: Marxian Explorations in Southern and Afro-American History* (New York, 1971), p. 201.
18. Alex Beam, "The Myth and the Man," *Boston Globe,* September 8, 1993, p. 15.
19. Arthur M. Schlesinger, Jr., "What the Thousand Days Wrought," *The New Republic,* November 21, 1983, p. 20.

SUGGESTED READING

No serious student of John F. Kennedy who travels to the Boston area should miss the user-friendly exhibits at the new museum at the John F. Kennedy Library at Columbia Point in Boston. The introductory film on JFK's life and times, 17 minutes in length, has JFK himself talking about the need to strip away myth from history. JFK would undoubtedly have been somewhat amused at the library's successful attempt to enshrine him in exactly the kind of heroic imagery and myth against which he himself had cautioned. The papers and oral history interviews with many of the major participants in the Kennedy years are housed in the library. Interested students should see Ronald E. Whealan, *Historical Materials in the John Fitzgerald Kennedy Library* (Boston: JFK Library, 1993) for a complete listing of the papers and materials held in the library. Access to each collection or oral history interview is determined by a separate agreement with the individuals who gave the facility their materials. While the museum is open to the public, students and researchers who wish to use the research facilities should write or call the library at 617-929-4534.

John F. Kennedy: The Early Years

The history of the Kennedy and Fitzgerald families is ably chronicled in Doris Kearns Goodwin, *The Fitzgeralds and the Kennedys: An American Saga* (New York: Simon and Schuster, 1987). Goodwin, using materials supplied by the Kennedy family, takes the reader right up to the inauguration in 1961. The story of John F. Kennedy's ambitious father is found in the excellent study by Richard J. Whalen, *The Founding Father: The Story of Joseph P. Kennedy* (New York: Signet, 1964). Not to be overlooked is the critical study of Kennedy's early years by Nigel Hamilton, *J.F.K.: Restless Youth* (New York: Random

House, 1992). While this history did not win many friends in Kennedy's family or inner circle, it is based on materials that the writer utilized in the Kennedy collection at the John F. Kennedy Library in Boston. For additional valuable insights into JFK's early life, Rose Fitzgerald Kennedy, *Times to Remember* (New York: Doubleday, 1974) has important anecdotal material—written, of course, from a mother's very biased and protective point of view.

The Boston Irish

No student of the life of John F. Kennedy can escape the amazing story of the rise to political and economic power of Boston's Irish citizens. For background on the Boston Irish see Oscar Handlin, *Boston's Immigrants* (New York: Atheneum, 1969) and the first-rate political biography by Jack Beatty, *The Rascal King: The Life and Times of James Michael Curley (1874–1958)* (Reading, Massachusetts: Addison Wesley, 1992). For what some critics call the best American novel about urban politics, see Edwin O'Connor, *The Last Hurrah* (Boston: Little, Brown, 1956). O'Connor's novel, a thinly veiled fictional account of the career of James Michael Curley, the legendary political enemy of the Kennedys, is already considered an American classic.

JFK: The War Years and Early Politics

Arthur Krock, *Memoirs: Sixty Years on the Firing Line* (New York: Funk and Wagnall's, 1968) contains interesting material on how JFK published his first book, *Why England Slept* (New York: Wilfred Funk, 1940). John F. Kennedy's military exploits are adequately covered in Robert J. Donovan, *PT-109: John F. Kennedy in World War II* (New York: McGraw Hill, 1961). JFK's early political career in Boston and his years in the House and Senate are examined in James MacGregor Burns, *John Kennedy: A Political Profile* (New York: Harcourt Brace, 1959).

The Election of 1960

The fascinating story of the election of 1960 is best told by Theodore H. White in his classic, *The Making of the President*

1960 (New York: Atheneum, 1961). This is the first and still the best book in what has become a quadrennial cottage industry. For additional insight into other aspects of that historic election, Lawrence H. Fuchs, *John F. Kennedy and American Catholicism* (New York: Meredith Press, 1967) is very important for contemporary students who may not understand the barriers that existed in national politics for Catholic Americans. For another perspective see Richard Nixon, *In the Arena: A Memoir of Victory, Defeat and Renewal* (New York: Simon and Schuster, 1990).

JFK, Cuba and the Bay of Pigs

For background into American involvement in Cuba, see Theodore Draper, *Castro's Revolution: Myths and Realities* (New York: Praeger, 1962) and Tad Szulc's excellent biography, *Fidel: A Critical Portrait* (New York: William Morrow, 1988). For the best and most detailed account of the Bay of Pigs fiasco see Peter Wyden, *Bay of Pigs: The Untold Story* (New York: Simon and Schuster, 1979).

The Kennedys and Civil Rights

The American civil rights movement has been well chronicled by historians in recent years. Among the most valuable studies that examine the relationship of the Kennedy brothers to civil rights are Taylor Branch, *Parting the Waters: America in the King Years* (New York: Simon and Schuster, 1988) and David J. Garrow, *Bearing the Cross: Martin Luther King, Jr., and the Southern Christian Leadership Conference* (New York: Vintage, 1986). David L. Lewis, *King: A Critical Biography* (Baltimore: Penguin, 1970) offers students a balanced but critical account of the life and career of the civil rights leader. For a valuable insight into the changing face of urban America, students should consult Nicholas Lemann, *The Promised Land: The Great Black Migration and How It Changed America* (New York: Vintage, 1992).

John F. Kennedy, Robert F. Kennedy, J. Edgar Hoover and the internal struggles over civil rights in the Department of Justice are detailed in the excellent study by Victor S. Navasky, *Kennedy Justice* (New York: Atheneum, 1971). Students should also consult Curt Gentry, *J. Edgar Hoover: The Man and the Secrets* (New York: Norton, 1991) and Anthony Summers, *Official and Confidential: The Secret Life of J. Edgar Hoover* (New York: Putnam, 1993) for insights into the powerful leader of the FBI who became the nemesis of the Kennedy brothers. The best study of Robert F. Kennedy to date is Arthur M. Schlesinger, Jr., *Robert Kennedy and His Times* (Boston: Houghton Mifflin, 1978).

The Cuban Missile Crisis

Robert F. Kennedy, *Thirteen Days: A Memoir of the Cuban Missile Crisis* (New York: Signet, 1969), offers the reader an exciting point of view of the crisis from one of the major participants in the event. Another participant's analysis is McGeorge Bundy, *Danger and Survival: Choices About the Bomb in the First Fifty Years* (New York: Random House, 1988). See especially Bundy's chapter "Khrushchev's Reasons and Why We Missed Them." The best historical accounts of the Cuban missile crisis can be found in Michael R. Beschloss, *The Crisis Years: Kennedy and Khrushchev 1960–1963* (New York: HarperCollins, 1991), Dino A. Brugoni, *Eyeball to Eyeball: The Inside Story of the Cuban Missile Crisis* (New York: Random House, 1991), and Robert Smith Thompson, *The Missiles of October: The Declassified Story of John F. Kennedy and the Cuban Missile Crisis* (New York: Simon and Schuster, 1992).

John F. Kennedy and Vietnam

A good place to begin the complex study of American involvement in Vietnam is with the early work of Bernard B. Fall, *The Two Viet-Nams: A Political and Military Analysis* (New York: Praeger, 1966). Fall, a journalist on the scene, was killed in Vietnam in 1967. The best overall scholarly treatments of Vietnam include Stanley Karnow, *Vietnam: A History* (New York: Viking, 1983) and Frances Fitzgerald, *Fire in the Lake: The Vietnamese and the Americans in Vietnam* (Boston: Atlantic-Little, Brown, 1972). The best study of the relationship between the Kennedy administration and events in Southeast Asia is David Halberstam, *The Best and the Brightest* (New York: Random House, 1972). For an excellent overview of

American foreign policy that led to Vietnam see Walter LaFeber, *America, Russia, and the Cold War 1945–1984* (New York: Knopf, 1985). Two recent valuable works dealing with JFK and Vietnam are William J. Rust, *Kennedy in Vietnam: American Vietnam Policy 1960–1963* (New York: Scribners, 1985) and John M. Newman, *JFK and Vietnam: Deception, Intrigue and the Struggle for Power* (New York: Warner Books, 1992).

The Kennedy Assassination

In confronting the maze of assassination theories—theories involving multiple and mysterious assassins, two Oswalds, multi-angled bullets doing magic tricks that defy the laws of physics, shadowy members of the Soviet KGB, mysterious Cubans, the Mafia, the FBI and CIA, entry wounds and/or exit wounds and a plethora of conspiracy theories—readers should approach the published materials with a very skeptical eye. Two essential works dealing with the Kennedy assassination are the *Report of the Warren Commission on the Assassination of President Kennedy* (New York: Bantam, 1964) and William Manchester, *The Death of a President, November, 1963* (New York: Harper and Row, 1967). Other interesting but differing theories include David S. Lifton, *Best Evidence: Disguise and Deception in the Assassination of John F. Kennedy* (New York: Macmillan, 1980), Henry Hurt, *Reasonable Doubt: An Investigation into the Assassination of John F. Kennedy* (New York: Henry Holt, 1985), Anthony Summers, *Conspiracy* (New York: Paragon House, 1989), and the Warren Commission's early critic Edward J. Epstein, whose three books—*Inquest* (New York: Viking, 1966), *Counterplot* (New York: Viking, 1969), and *Legend: The Secret World of Lee Harvey Oswald* (New York: Ballantine, 1978)—have been recently republished in one volume, *The Assassination Chronicles* (New York: Carroll & Graf, 1992). Though published too late to be utilized in this book, Gaeton Fonzi's *The Last Investigation* (New York: Thunder's Mouth Press, 1994) is a remarkable and courageous study that sheds much-needed light on the inner workings of the House Committee on Assassinations. Fonzi, a Philadelphia and Miami-based investigative reporter, was a special investigator for the House Committee. His work points clearly in the direction of a conspiracy deep within the bowels of the Central

Intelligence Agency. To come full circle, students should see Gerald Posner, *Case Closed: Lee Harvey Oswald and the Assassination of JFK* (New York: Random House, 1993).

John F. Kennedy and the Press

Two valuable studies of the interesting relationship between JFK and the expanding and changing print and electronic media are Montague Kern, Patricia W. Levering and Ralph B. Levering, *The Kennedy Crises: The Press, the Presidency, and Foreign Policy* (Chapel Hill: University of North Carolina, 1983) and Mary Ann Watson, *The Expanding Vista: American Television in the Kennedy Years* (New York: Oxford, 1990).

Insiders' Views

Two books by Kennedy insiders are indispensable to any study of the Kennedy administration. Historian Arthur M. Schlesinger, Jr., *A Thousand Days: John F. Kennedy in the White House* (Boston: Houghton Mifflin, 1965) has provided students with the most valuable history to date of the view from inside the administration. Schlesinger was a special assistant to the president. Speechwriter and adviser Theodore Sorensen's *Kennedy* (New York: Harper and Row, 1965) is also excellent. Other valuable books include Kenneth P. O'Donnell and David F. Powers with Joe McCarthy, *"Johnny, We Hardly Knew Ye": Memories of John Fitzgerald Kennedy* (New York: Pocket Books, 1973), Paul B. Fay, *The Pleasure of His Company* (New York: Harper and Row, 1966), Pierre Salinger, *With Kennedy* (Garden City, New York: Doubleday, 1966), and Benjamin C. Bradlee, *Conversations With Kennedy* (New York: Pocket Books, 1976). Bradlee, the former editor of the *Washington Post,* was one of many journalists cultivated over the years by John F. Kennedy who became a personal friend.

Biographies and History

Kennedy scholarship falls into two camps: the supporters and the critics. When John F. Kennedy was assassinated, Victor Lasky's *JFK: The Man and the Myth* (New York: Macmillan, 1963) was on the best-seller lists. Because of its anti-Kennedy point of view it soon disappeared and has been out of print for many years. However, by the 1970s a number of important studies critical of the Kennedy years appeared. Among the best are Henry Fairlie, *The Kennedy Promise: The Politics of Expectation* (Garden City, New York: Doubleday, 1973), Joan and Clay Blair, Jr., *The Search for J.F.K.* (New York: Berkley Putnam, 1976), and Lewis J. Paper, *John F. Kennedy: The Promise and the Performance* (New York: Da Capo, 1979). The most recent critical study of Kennedy, which sums up much of the work of the critics, is a work by historian Thomas C. Reeves, entitled *A Question of Character: A Life of John F. Kennedy* (New York: Free Press, 1991).

Among the studies that see John F. Kennedy in a more positive light are Hugh Sidey, *John F. Kennedy, President* (New York: Atheneum, 1964), Herbert S. Parmet, *JFK: The Presidency of John F. Kennedy* (New York: Dial Press, 1983), Irving Bernstein, *Promises Kept: John F. Kennedy's New Frontier* (New York: Oxford, 1991), and James N. Giglio, *The Presidency of John F. Kennedy* (Lawrence: University Press of Kansas, 1991).

The best overall study, and the most balanced account of the Kennedy presidency to appear thus far, is Richard Reeves, *President Kennedy: Profile of Power* (New York: Simon and Schuster, 1993). Reeves does not hesitate to criticize the fallen president. But at the same time he offers the reader an insightful inside view of the difficulties faced by the young president and of his accomplishments in these trying years. No Kennedy student should overlook the especially valuable book by Leo Damore, *The Cape Cod Years of John F. Kennedy* (Englewood Cliffs, New Jersey: Prentice Hall, 1967) for an in-depth insight into how the Kennedy family spent their summers, and into the important role played by Cape Cod in JFK's life from 1926 to his election in 1960.

Jacqueline Kennedy Onassis

The late widow of President Kennedy jealously guarded the Kennedy myth and legend, as well as her own privacy. She granted only two interviews after she left the White House. Neither has been published. Her papers covering the years 1963–1968 are at the Kennedy Library in Boston. A 1974 oral history interview has been deposited at the Lyndon Baines Johnson Library in Austin, Texas. Among the many books written about this beautiful and dignified former First Lady, few have any lasting scholarly value. The one consulted for this study is C. David Heymann, *A Woman Named Jackie: An Intimate Biography of Jacqueline Bouvier Kennedy Onassis* (New York: Lyle Stuart, 1989). Her untimely death in 1994 will undoubtedly leave a major gap in our knowledge of John F. Kennedy's most intimate and crucial years.

The United States in the Twentieth Century

John F. Kennedy was the first president to be born in this century. His life spanned two world wars, the Great Depression, the New Deal and the first 18 years of the Cold War. The following works provide background to the life and times of John F. Kennedy:

John Kenneth Galbraith, *The Great Crash 1929* (Boston: Houghton Mifflin, 1961) is an excellent account of the beginning of the Great Depression. David Halberstam, *The Fifties* (New York: Villard Books, 1993) shows that the Eisenhower years were far from boring. Eric F. Goldman, *The Crucial Decade—and After: America, 1945–1960* (New York: Vintage, 1960) provides an excellent background and prelude to the Kennedy years. David A. Shannon, *Twentieth Century America: The United States Since the 1890's* (Chicago: Rand McNally, 1963) takes the reader through all of the years in which Kennedy lived, and closes in 1962. Malcolm Shaw, editor, *The Modern Presidency: From Roosevelt to Reagan* (New York: Harper and Row, 1987) is a valuable collection of essays on the evolution of the modern presidency.

INDEX

Boldface page numbers indicate main topics.
Italic page numbers indicate illustrations.

A

Acheson, Dean 75, 110
Adams, Henry 32
Adams, John 32
Adams, John Quincy 32
Addison's disease 37, 49–50, 151
Alabama
  campus integration 101–102, 104
  "freedom rides" 99
  police racism 99–100
Alabama, University of 101–102
Aleman, Don Miguel 47
"All politics is local" 2
American Revolution 49
American Strategic Air Command 114
American Weekly 56
Anderson Jr., Rudolf 109
Anniston (Alabama) 99
anti-Semitism 11–12, 71
appeasement 10–12, 14
Arvad, Inga 19, 92
As We Remember Joe (John F. Kennedy) 24
Atlanta (Georgia) 96
Auchincloss, Hugh D. 46, 47
autopsy reports 142

B

Baez, Joan 102
Baldwin, James 101
Ball, George 110
banking 3
Barnett, Ross 97

Batista, Fulgencio 76
Bay of Pigs invasion **74–88,** 107, 109, 113, 128, 153
Beam, Alex 154
Beatty, Jack 35
Belafonte, Harry 102
Bentsen, Lloyd xiv
Berlin (Germany) 107–108, 111
Berlin Olympics (1936) 19
Berlin Wall 108, 153
Bernstein, Irving 152
Bible 95
Bickel, Alexander 91
"Big Minh" *see* Minh, Duong Van ("Big Minh")
Billings, K. LeMoyne ("Lem") 8–10, 25, 39, 47
Biltmore Hotel (Los Angeles, California) 64
Birmingham (Alabama) 99
Bissell, Richard 77, 84
black Americans
  in civil rights movement *see* civil rights
  as JFK supporters 70, 104–105
  poverty of 89–90
  rioting by 104
Blair Jr., Clay 151
Blair, Joan 151
Boggs, Hale 39
Bohlen, George 110
Bond, Julian 96
Book-of-the-Month Club 14
Boston (Massachusetts)
  JFK congressional campaign (1946) 24–25, 27–34

B
Kennedy
G

Goldman, Martin S. 1795

John F. Kennedy,
   portrait of a
   president.

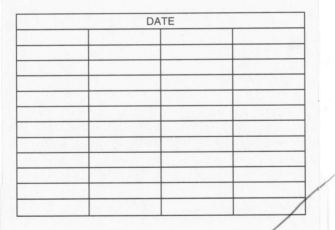

DATE			